AF598745

MEMOIRS *of a* HIGH PRIEST

The Life and Majick of ALEXANDER CABOT

BY ALEXANDER CABOT
Foreword by Laurie Cabot
Afterthoughts by Sorita d'Este

4880 Lower Valley Road, Atglen, PA 19310

Library of Congress Control Number: 2025930656

Disclaimer: All of the information detailed herein originates from personal magickal practices and from the author's own viewpoint and personal recollection of historical events. No names have been intentionally changed, and all events are accurately portrayed according to the author's memory.

Compiling editor for previous edition Laila Florane
Copy and content editor David Moore
Cover photography for previous edition Ieva Sireikyte
Designed by Jack Chappell
Cover design by Danielle Farmer
Type set in Salden/Garamond

ISBN: 978-0-7643-7015-1
ePub: 978-1-5073-0589-8
Printed in China

10 9 8 7 6 5 4 3 2 1

Published by REDFeather Mind, Body, Spirit
An imprint of Schiffer Publishing, Ltd.
4880 Lower Valley Road
Atglen, PA 19310
Phone: (610) 593-1777; Fax: (610) 593-2002
Email: Info@redfeathermbs.com
Web: www.redfeathermbs.com

For our complete selection of fine books on this and related subjects, please visit our website at www.redfeathermbs.com. You may also write for a free catalog.

We are always looking for people to write books on new and related subjects. If you have an idea for a book, please contact us at proposals@schifferbooks.com.

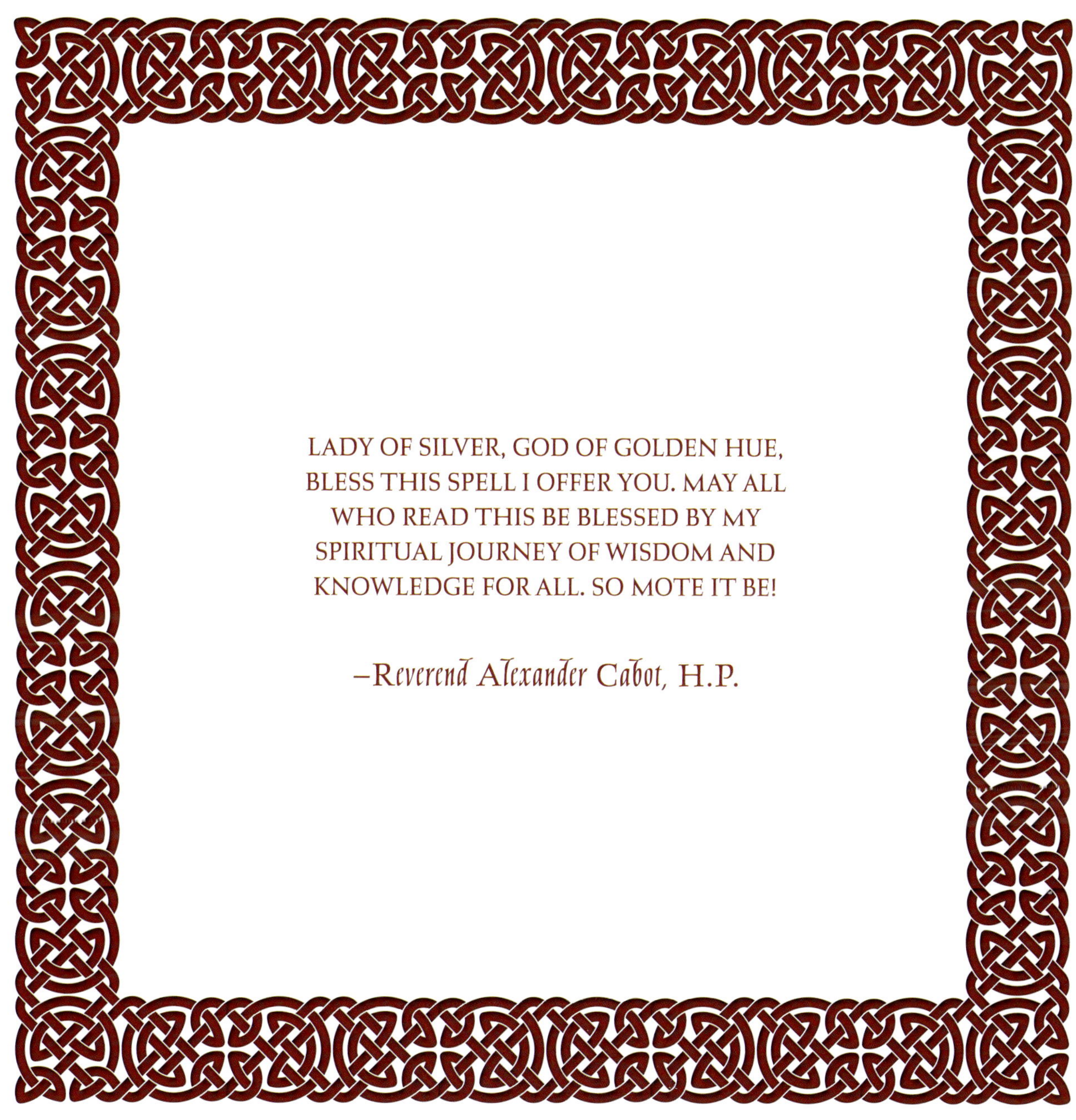

LADY OF SILVER, GOD OF GOLDEN HUE,
BLESS THIS SPELL I OFFER YOU. MAY ALL
WHO READ THIS BE BLESSED BY MY
SPIRITUAL JOURNEY OF WISDOM AND
KNOWLEDGE FOR ALL. SO MOTE IT BE!

–Reverend Alexander Cabot, H.P.

From his birth in Havana, Cuba, Alexander was destined to perform wonderous works of love and spirit, shining blessings far and wide from his new home in New York. The Goddess claimed him from the beginning, and with her kiss of approval, his spiritual journey began. From the days of the Magickal Childe and Enchantments, I've seen his life and spiritual discoveries unfold, and his heart has always been linked to the Great Mother. When I gave him the name Lord Hekatos, an epithet to Apollo, he embodied that God of Light well but always knew he was a secret child of the Goddess. He has been respectful of and in service to his High Priestesses, recognizing them as avatars of his Lady. More than merely respectful, he has always been generous with his time, love, and devotion.

As a good representative of the divine, even as a young man, his behavior was always impeccable in my view. He always left people with new things to ponder, new viewpoints, and new appreciations of the craft. I have really enjoyed my journey with my High Priest, brother, and friend. One of the beautiful things about the following memoirs is that we can all see a part of our own spiritual connection to the divine in his story.

Let us join hands as we turn these magick pages together, in love and trust. The circle is open, but never broken. So mote it be.

—Lady Rhea, author of *The Enchanted Candle* and *The Enchanted Formulary*

(Photo by Richard Santana)

"Alexander Cabot's *Memoirs of a High Priest: The Life and Majick of Alexander Cabot* is a memoir of his journey into the world of magick and witchcraft from childhood to adulthood. The book is heartfelt, entertaining, and insightful (all of which are great reasons to read this book). Unlike other informative books on magick and witchcraft that focus on techniques or theories, Alexander's memoirs relay magickal knowledge in a delightful way! The knowledge is given in a kind of choreographed manner. At times, it feels like the reader, who is seeing Alexander's journey as he acquired his magickal power, is engaging with a captivating script of a marvelous play! Some things are best learned and understood by seeing the story unfold (either on the written page or in person). Regardless of which path you follow or where you are in your journey, this book will offer you encouragement and insight. On a personal note: both Alexander and I were born in Cuba, and we both immigrated to the United States. While reading his memoirs, I was intrigued to learn of the similarities and the differences in how we came to be witches."

—Ivo Dominguez Jr., author of *Keys to Perception*; *Casting Sacred Space*; *Practical Astrology for Witches and Pagans*; *Spirit Speak: Knowing and Understanding Spirit Guides, Ancestors, Ghosts, Angels, and the Divine*; and *The Four Elements of the Wise*

"*Memoirs of a High Priest: The Life and Majick of Alexander Cabot* is a heartfelt and inspiring memoir of a man who has dedicated his life to Spirit, the pursuit of magical practice, and service to his community. Alexander shares personal stories, the history of his magickal life, and informative material on the traditions he holds dear. This book chronicles his journey, from his family fleeing Cuba during Fidel Castro's reign to his exploration of a list of magickal traditions. His path eventually led him to live the honorable service role to the magickal community as a High Priest and an Emissary and Elder of the Craft of the Wise. This book is truly a fascinating read!"

—Mickie Mueller, author of *The Witch's Mirror: The Craft, Lore & Magick of the Looking Glass*

"There is a difference between wanting to be a witch because it seems cool and being called to be a witch, priest, or priestess of the Goddess. For the former there is always choice; however, for the latter, no. When the Goddess calls to a person and that call is answered, the veils fall like dominos, revealing an unfolding path that may be filled with sacrifice and even loneliness yet is also filled with magick, adventure, and much love. *Memoirs of a High Priest: The Life and Majick of Alexander Cabot* is honest and deeply personal, recounting a journey showing what it truly means to be chosen by the Goddess and to heed her call. Written with much sincerity and humility, it is little wonder She claimed Alexander to be one of her own. Not only is this book truly a mesmerizing read, but it offers a guide for all priests and priestesses who the Goddess touches."

—Frances Billinghurst, author of *Dancing the Sacred Wheel*; *Encountering the Dark Goddess: A Journey into the Shadow Realms;* and *Contemporary Witchcraft: Foundational Practices for a Magical Life* and editor of *Call of the God: An Anthology Exploring the Divine Masculine within Modern Paganism*

"In this book, *Memoirs of a High Priest: The Life and Majick of Alexander Cabot*, Reverend Alexander Cabot offers a beautiful, sincere, unique, and enchanting book. It truly stands out as a memoir of magick and witchcraft.

Over the years, I have had the pleasure of knowing many fine High Priests, who have penned their knowledge and wisdom in the hopes that seekers would benefit from those teachings, but sadly, it is rare to hear of one writing about the more private aspects of their personal journeys and studies. Alexander does this masterfully in this work! He also speaks of the wise women who have revealed to him the subtle curvatures in the living presence of the Goddess.

One of the special gifts Alexander provides is background information, including relevant history, a personal view of Afro-Cuban practices, and an inside look at working with spirits. This book also shares a truly rare gift, as it is a glimpse into the thoughts, feelings, defining experiences, and magickal meanderings of a boy who becomes a witch, growing up to become a High Priest to one of the most famous witches in the world, Laurie Cabot. Behind it all was the Queen of all Witcheries—the Great Goddess, 'whose body encircles the universe,' who touched his soul and inspired his lessons and journeys."

—Orion Foxwood, elder of Traditional Witchcraft, Faery Seer, and Conjurer in Southern Folk; author of *The Flame in the Caldron* and *The Tree of Enchantment*; and founder of the House of Brigh Faery Seership Institute

"Fascinating autobiographical read of one man's journey and heritage—a truly unique narrative of a life laced with incredible psychic energy. He captivates us, from breaking a family curse to his amazing experiences in various occult disciplines. Told with grace and elegance, Alexander Cabot embraces us with his powerful story, filled with vibrant enchantment, power, wisdom, and inspiration. A jewel of a read!"

—Silver Ravenwolf, best-selling author of *To Ride a Silver Broomstick* and lecturer on Pagan and Witchcraft topics

"*Memoirs of a High Priest: The Life and Majick of Alexander Cabot* is a wonderful book that I highly recommend. It is the autobiography of Reverend High Priest Alexander Cabot, Lord Hekatos, one of the most important High Priests of one of the most important Traditions of Witchcraft, the Cabot Tradition. The book is a deceptively easy read, for despite its straightforward narration, it is stuffed with important information, some of which may not be available anywhere else. In *Memoirs of a High Priest*, Reverend Alexander recounts his personal journey, beginning as a child of a Cuban American family with a strong metaphysical background, and taking him through Spiritualism, Santeria, Welsh Traditional Witchcraft, Gardnerian–New York Wicca, and finally the Cabot Tradition itself. In telling this story, he creates a snapshot of the metaphysical community of New York and the Northeast in the 1980s and 1990s, which is invaluable to students of the history of our community. Alexander recounts local and global adventures, as well as experiences with such historical figures as Herman Slater, Eddie Buczynski, Lady Rhea, and of course Laurie Cabot. Chapter 8 includes a lovely introduction to the Cabot Tradition for those who are unfamiliar with it. I must say that, for me personally, the most fascinating part of the book is the part that deals with Alexander's childhood and family, the world of metaphysical Cuba, and the beautifully imparted story of what it is like to grow up as a magickal child. Again, I highly recommend *Memoirs of a High Priest: The Life and Majick of Alexander Cabot* to anyone with an interest in metaphysics and the history of the metaphysical community."

—M. Reverend Don Lewis-Highcorrell, more commonly known as Reverend Don Lewis, chancellor of the Correllian Tradition, cofounder of Witch School International. Reverend Lewis has been an initiated priest since 1976, and he became a High Priest in 1979. Among his copious list of works, he edited several Pagan publications in the past and regularly writes and produces Pagan video content today. He designed the *Tarot of Hekate* in 1982, and he is a font of wisdom and knowledge on the craft of the wise.

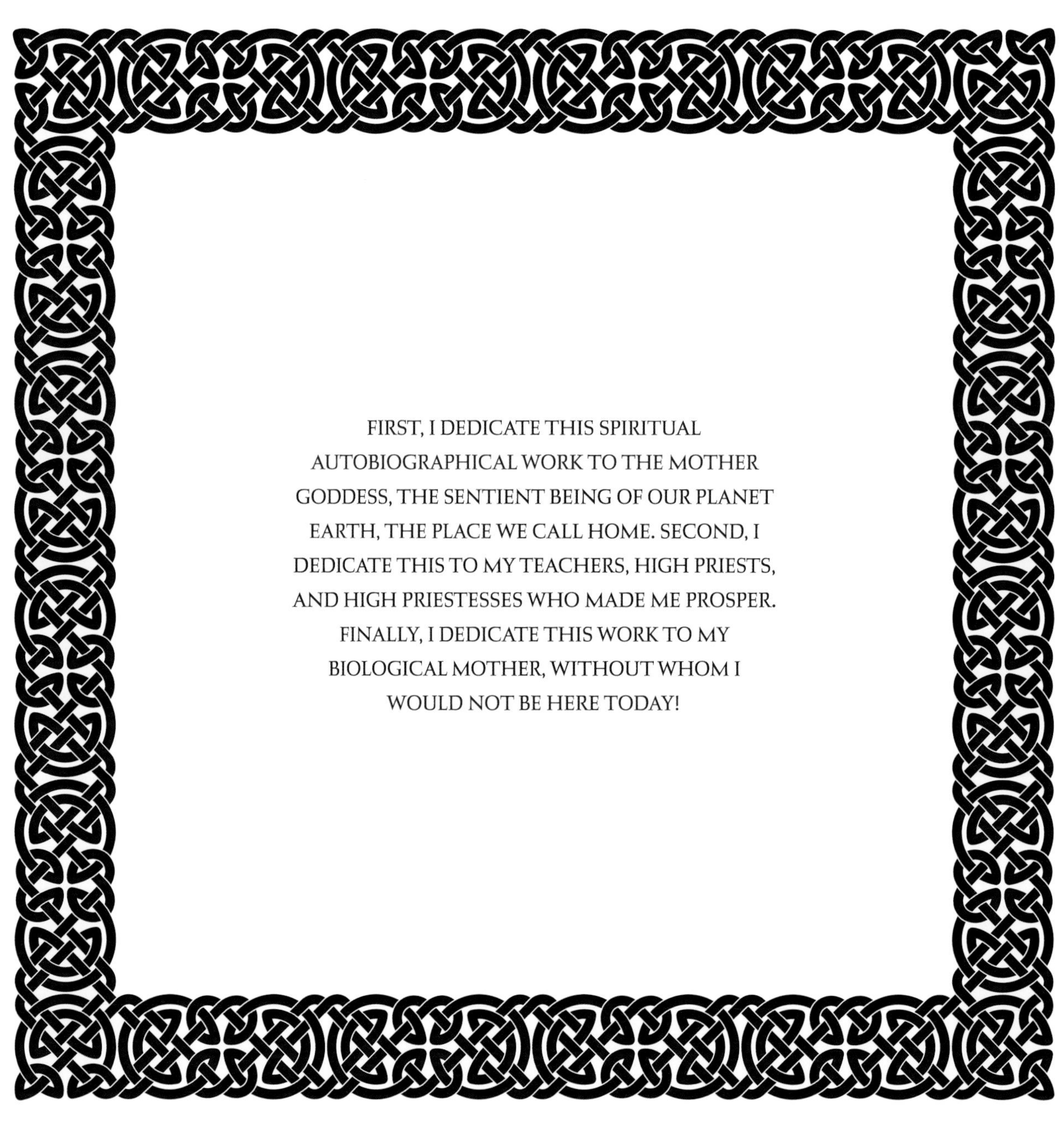

FIRST, I DEDICATE THIS SPIRITUAL AUTOBIOGRAPHICAL WORK TO THE MOTHER GODDESS, THE SENTIENT BEING OF OUR PLANET EARTH, THE PLACE WE CALL HOME. SECOND, I DEDICATE THIS TO MY TEACHERS, HIGH PRIESTS, AND HIGH PRIESTESSES WHO MADE ME PROSPER. FINALLY, I DEDICATE THIS WORK TO MY BIOLOGICAL MOTHER, WITHOUT WHOM I WOULD NOT BE HERE TODAY!

ACKNOWLEDGMENTS

I am deeply honored by Laurie Cabot, my High Priestess, and I am honored to share the legacy of the Cabot Tradition, an important part of my journey.

My gratitude goes to Lady Rhea, one of my dearest friends. I am most appreciative for your continued love and support. It was you who ignited in me a passion for writing by giving me the privilege of contributing to your published works. It was because of this passion that I decided to contribute my own work to the community I hold dear.

I am honored and grateful for Sorita d'Este for her contributions and loving support always.

I am also deeply grateful to Laila Florane for her immense contributions to this work. Her passion for my legacy, her guidance, and her knowledge of history and the written word helped piece together this beautiful tapestry of my life's journeys.

And to David Moore, my brother of honor, protection, and guidance, I appreciate your talents in editing my book, for helping write the expanded American edition, and for ensuring that my written memoirs have the proper flow and function needed for optimum reading.

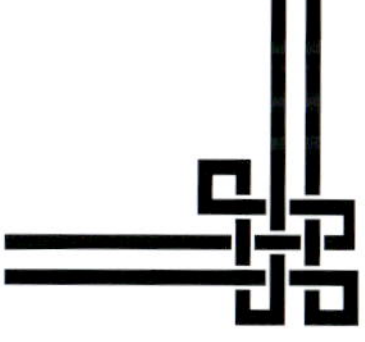

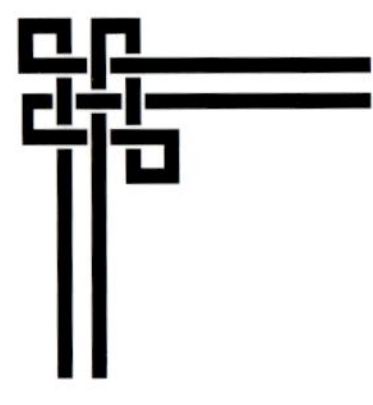

CONTENTS

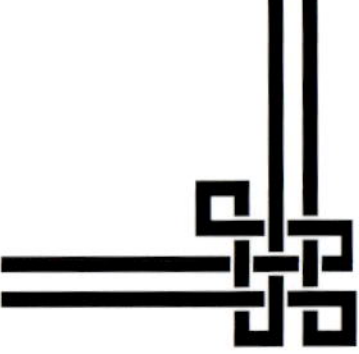

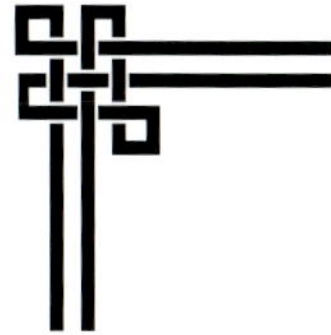

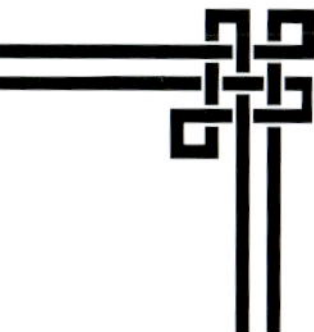

FOREWORD

BY LAURIE CABOT

As children, the vastness of our universe seems unknowable and often even hostile. We feel small and insignificant, no matter our beginnings. There is often a spirit guiding us along the majickal path to enlightenment. Sometimes the spirit is a predestined legacy of our majickal heritage being programmed into a child's mind, at times through play and frequently through dreams. From birth, Alexander has lent a way for spirit and consciousness from the universe to lead him as he progressed toward his destiny as an ambassador of majick, a High Priest of witchcraft, through his studies, his practices, and his innate knowledge of majick to become a beacon, leader, and protector. He is now the highest of all clergy in a tradition of witchcraft known as the Cabot Tradition.

It's fair to say that I am one who is well acquainted with the Craft. I founded the Cabot Tradition in the hopes of sharing the majickal wisdom of the Celts, the ancient ones, and I am a lifelong follower of the Hermetic mystery schools. I teach Hermetic science, with modern science blended in to reinforce the understanding of the principles. This pragmatic approach is the cornerstone of my Cabot Tradition of Witchcraft. My goal is to inform students of the Craft about the importance of individual sovereignty, and also the importance of working in harmony with Mother Nature and understanding her energies. I enjoy showing students how witchcraft helps us to gain a deeper understanding of cutting-edge science, and how science gives us a deeper appreciation for witchcraft, rather than the two philosophies being mutually exclusive. Witches are the stewards of this planet and all who dwell upon it.

The Cabot Kent Hermetic Temple was the first federally recognized temple of witchcraft in Salem, Massachusetts. I worked hard for most of my life to create a legacy that would train great men and women to become influential High Priests and High Priestesses, and Alexander is one of those great men, without a doubt. He has worked tirelessly for decades to master his own craft and to help and teach others, and you may now have a window into his beginnings, his influences, and his processes. What a treat!

In this book, Alexander takes readers along on his journey of learning, through many different cultures and traditions. From birth, he was an instrument of the divine, and he broke a curse with his first breath. He was designed from the beginning to be a blessing, and his parents could sense his innate abilities before he was born. His entire family was spiritual, and many of them were powerful practitioners of the majickal arts. From his experience with Freemasonry, and Catholicism and their saints, to his grandmother and her majickal herbalism, along with his studies and adventures with alchemy, Palo Mayombe, Santeria/Lucumi, and many more disciplines, the adventure is exciting to share. Alexander is still using his wide knowledge of majick to honor his heritage and to expand his priesthood with the Cabot Tradition as he travels the world, helping to heal the earth and all upon it, and to guide others to do the same. We are proud that he represents us as our Cabot Ambassador to Brazil, and I am deeply honored to be represented everywhere he goes by someone so genuinely good.

I've enjoyed many moments of sitting with Alexander and chatting over tea, learning about all of his wonderful life experiences. I hope you will enjoy traveling through time with Alexander as much as I have. This book is a lovely read and an enrapturing journey that you surely will enjoy.

~ Reverend High Priestess Laurie Cabot

The Reverend High Priestess Laurie Cabot has written many books, such as *The Power of the Witch* and *Laurie Cabot's Book of Shadows*. Founder of her own tradition and temple, she has been recognized as the "Official Witch of Salem," receiving the State of Massachusetts' Patriot Award in the mid-'70s (presented by Michael S. Dukakis, then governor of Massachusetts) for her public service, especially for working with special-needs children. She has been interviewed by some of the most renowned media outlets (such as *National Geographic*) for her extraordinary accomplishments. One of the most iconic witches of our modern age, she continues to teach and share wisdom as of the writing of this book, and she is widely loved and revered among witches and nonwitches alike.

Teatime with the Cabot Tradition (photo by Dawn C. Dorgan)

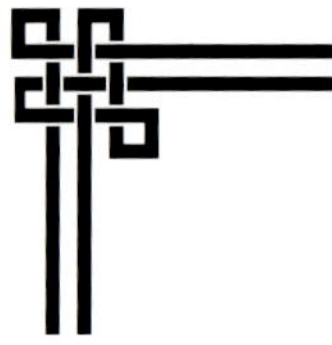

PROLOGUE

APRIL 16, 1961

Fidel Castro and his revolution had to be stopped. The United States decided to do just that. Approximately 1,500 exiled Cubans (backed by the Central Intelligence Agency) invaded Cuba via the Bay of Pigs. Outcome: This would prove to be an epic defeat. The Soviet Union now had an even-firmer grip on Cuba. Would some of Cuba's magickal people escape the oppression?

It has been a dream of mine to write a book detailing my magickal heritage. (Magick, spelled with a "k," comes from Aleister Crowley, since he intended to differentiate between stage magicians and the occult sciences. This remains a popular spelling today.) My hope is that you will journey back with me and, through my experiences, touch the Divine Mother, the Goddess, who writes my destiny and yours. She is ever present. Will you reach for her?

We all have a common heritage, connected through Spirit and Nature; we therefore have a right to all human culture. It is an honor to share with you my personal spiritual history, rich with occult knowledge and practice, beginning with my close biological family.

Salvador and Alida (my mom and dad) Havana, Cuba, 1962

My story began before I did, so that is where we will start. I hope you will enjoy meeting my beloved family and mentors. Take my hand as I introduce you to my magickal life.

MI PADRE

My father, Salvador, was the embodiment of the spirit, protector, and savior. He was bold and courageous, willing to do what was right to shield his family and his people.

He always hoped against hope that the much-anticipated Bay of Pigs mission would result in historic triumph. His passion for the cause was so great that he decided to join the underground dissident party, which had been created to overthrow the Communist administration set in place. My father, along with many others, had been blinded by Fidel Castro's charisma at first. It was now clear, however, that Castro was out of his sheep's clothing, and his narcissistic appetite was ferocious. Castro was a practitioner of magick. I was told that he had a slew of priests and necromancers who worked for him, including Santeros, Santeras, Babalawos, and Paleros. He chose to deal in the dark arts to further his goals, and according to reports he was able to avoid more than ten assassination attempts and many magickal attacks from his enemies. The word was that he had many spirits enslaved to protect him and his home, and to keep his government strong.

Dad ached with the memory of Havana, his home, prior to the revolution. Under Castro, residents of Havana underwent harsh living conditions, including rationing and limited freedom. My father knew that he and his family deserved to be free of such tyranny. The only hope for Havana at the time was for the United States to intervene, to overthrow the evil of Castro's government. That was certainly my father's hope. Much to his dismay, US president John F. Kennedy's administration bailed out at the last minute; the Air Force that was promised never materialized. This resulted in the death of many men who sought to bring democracy to their native land.

My father was now burdened with the worry of being targeted among the many dissidents abroad and in Cuba, and he could have been killed. Luckily, that didn't happen, and he was able to go on with life, meeting my mother and eventually living a life filled with freedom, opportunity, and the hope a democratic republic brings.

As a sidenote, Cuba was previously under a "dictablanda," a colloquial word meaning "bland dictatorship." This was due to the efforts of Fulgencio Batista. Batista was a Cuban military officer and politician who served as the elected president of Cuba from 1940 to 1944, and who later lost an election but took over as a military dictator (with US backing) for seven more years. He would lift up the country to global recognition as a mix of paradise and corruption. Batista reigned for two terms, and it was he who opened Havana to be more than what it had been, "the Paris of the Caribbean," called that for its beautiful architecture, vibrant arts scene, and flourishing nightlife. However, this was far from perfect. This new government, like so many other countries, failed to address the needs of those in poverty and the illiteracy problems suffered by many people. Despite all of its corrupt failures, Batista's dictatorship successfully gave some strength to Cuba's infrastructure and fostered some significant economic growth.

MI MADRE

My mother, Alida, who had poliomyelitis, was born into a large family (she was one of thirteen siblings). Her family was all that she knew. She never imagined that one day she would be forced to leave that family and would have to start anew in a different country.

In the early 1960s, Alida fell in love with my father. His family differed from hers, in that his was cultured and refined, and also wealthy. She was an outsider to them, a farmer's daughter with a fourth-grade education. She certainly was unfamiliar with the ways of his higher class of society. My father's family, for a time, looked past that. She was praised for her beauty (a reflection of the Goddess within and without). It was decided that Alida was to be granted an official wedding, which was a really big deal, and something that some others in Salvador's family disapproved of strongly. (Note: Although privileged, my father's family's resources were greatly lessened by the Communist regime of the 1960s, so large expenses were often a source of friction and contention.)

As it turned out, my mother's beauty and honored privilege with the aforementioned wedding would lead to powerful jealousy and deceit. One of my father's relatives developed a strong resentment toward Alida. Her resentment grew so strong that she felt she had to do something to get rid of my mom, so this relative hired a palero (a necromancer/priest of the religion Palo, a syncretic religion formed by the Congo slaves who had settled in Cuba) who cursed my mother with a demented spirit. This spirit caused her to become reclusive and depressed. It was done without the knowledge of anyone other than the palero and the malevolent relative.

Not too long afterward, my mother suffered her first miscarriage, who would have been my older sister today. Years later, this lost sister manifested herself in a séance (*misa espiritual*). During the séance, my sister's spirit gave the account of the relative's deceit, and how, had it not been for the evil workings of the necromancer, my sister would have been able to be born and thrive in the realm of the living. The words of my late sister were later confirmed by my grandmother, who provided the historical details.

After the devastating miscarriage, my mother suffered severe depression. Eventually, my father was successful in helping her to relieve her anxiety. Months later, under an old moon (waning crescent) in Havana, I was born with the ability to counteract the demented spirit's energy. (I have since noticed within this plane of existence that I do possess the natural power of spirit mediumship and exorcism.)

Alida, Havana, Cuba, 1962

The wicked family member's evil intent to get rid of my mom was thusly defeated, counteracted by the continued love and devotion of my father to my mother and by the Goddess granting her a child gifted with the power of exorcism at birth. There is no power in the universe stronger than Love.

HER STORY OF OUR EXODUS

My mother, like so many who survived the tyranny of Castro's dictatorship, suffered a kind of posttraumatic stress disorder (PTSD). It is common for war veterans to suffer PTSD and for them to recount many years afterward the traumatic events that led to them getting this disorder, but my mother kept her trauma silent for many years.

It was not until Thanksgiving, November 24, 2016, that my mother finally recounted the story of our family's exodus from Cuba to the United States to me in full. Interestingly enough, unknown to any of us at the time, Castro died the day after. (My belief is that my mother was feeling the weight of Castro's strong, psychic energy fading away, and that's why she finally had the courage to speak up about the detailed events of our family leaving Cuba as he was dying.)

Everyone knew that the militia would come and do an inventory of their home, including all of their possessions, should they decide to be a part of the exodus. People were able to leave with only one suitcase, their wedding ring, some of their clothing, and their personal documents. (Prior to the inventory, many people evacuating Cuba would donate their belongings—such as blenders and other small items—to family members who stayed behind. The militia would look only for bare essentials, such as furniture, when people would leave.)

With sadness, my mother recounted that on the day we left, my father was forced to stay behind. He was twenty-eight years of age. It was mandatory for him to serve time in the militia. (Castro had declared that anyone who was not in favor of the revolution may leave. However, after the numbers grew to be too great, he decided to stop the mass exodus in 1971.)

My father held me, a sixteen-month-old toddler, in his arms. Then the militia ripped me out of his arms to give me to my mother. I cried for my father! It would solely be up to my mother to care for me from then on.

We were escorted into a car that was also supposed to transport my grandparents, but they were forced to use another car. The public onlookers screamed, "Gusano!" (this translates to *worms*). "Worms, get out! Antirevolutionaries!" they said as they threw eggs and rocks in our direction.

My mother and I were taken to a concentration camp. We were not allowed to communicate with my paternal grandparents. During the late-night hours there, Mom said that she did all that she could to console me. I was crying hysterically because of the loud gunshots that sounded periodically throughout the night. I did not understand the alarming bangs. It's a good thing I had no idea that a firing squad was tasked with constantly executing dissidents into the wee hours of the morning, but maybe even at that age, I was feeling the horror of the mass murders.

There were two airlines used to escort evacuees from Cuba to the mainland United States and Puerto Rico: Pan Am and Cubana. The night after our stay in the concentration camp, my mother and I boarded Pan Am to Miami, the check-in point for those like us. As it turned out, my grandparents had been delayed a day from traveling out, and my aunt and cousin were deliberately sent to Madrid, Spain. The regiment, under Castro, was busy separating families, just like what had happened to many Jews under Nazi rule. We were what others would eventually call the "Jews of the Caribbean."

Me and mom, Thanksgiving, November 24, 2016

SETTLEMENT

From the airport in Miami, we were taken to the Liberty Tower, an old colonial building that is now owned and operated by the Cuban American Foundation. It was a center where refugees had to register and pass through once arriving in the States.

My mother and I were sponsored by my paternal grandfather who lived in Queens, New York. So, after our brief stay in Miami, where we received a small amount of money, we traveled to Queens to be with my grandfather. We arrived in New York unprepared for the weather, since it was snowing and I was in shorts. I was freezing. A kindly flight attendant gave my mother a Pan Am blanket to cover me, and I have that blanket to this day. It was the first time my mother or I had seen snow!

After we had been in Queens a couple of months, we were told that there were jobs available nearby in a thriving Cuban American community. Much like Miami's Little Havana, it was called Havana on the Hudson. This was the second immigration concentration, located right across the river from Manhattan. There were adjacent cities, such as Union City and West New York, where the bulk of Cuban immigrants lived. This Hudson County area was made up of a majority of Italians, with a minority of Irish and German workers, and with the arrival of Cuban immigrants in the '60s, a lot of friction existed. The racist, xenophobic behavior; the depressed economic conditions; and the struggles people faced in their everyday lives made for a somewhat hostile environment. We had to band together to remain safe, and with language and cultural differences, we became a close-knit community. We have always been a very hardworking people, known to be productive and often making ourselves successful. Soon, there were many locally owned Cuban businesses. Bergenline Avenue, which spans a large area in North Hudson County, especially flourished with Cuban business activity.

EARLY CHILDHOOD

I grew up with the mentality of freethinkers, due to my lineage—my grandfathers, father, and uncles were Masons. My mother was a daughter of the Order of the Eastern Star. (The Order of the Eastern Star was a Masonic organization created by a Mason, Rob Morris, in 1850. Unlike the Free and Accepted Masons, the Order of the Eastern Star is open to both women and men, although it is primarily composed of women.)

At home, I was surrounded with the presence of female divinity. It was very prominent because my mother revered only one saint, and that was Saint Barbara, a Grecian martyr. Saint Barbara's feast day each year is December 4. She is one of the "Fourteen Holy Helpers," auxillary saints honored each August 8 for their incredible intercessory powers, especially for battling sickness. Saint Barbara is often seen with a tower and chains. My mother kept one home altar that featured Saint Barbara. On the altar, there was a red apple, a red rose, and a red candle. Saint Barbara embodied both the Divine Feminine and Divine Masculine energies in my home (I recall myself, in my youth, praying to St. Barbara to successfully pass my exams). Saint Barbara was syncretized with Chango, a male Orisha with similar attributes. Both are associated with the colors red and white and with electrical storms.

While Saint Barbara was my mom's divine feminine at home, I was more drawn toward "La Milagrosa," the Virgin Mary, due to my Catholic upbringing. She spoke to me as my own personal connection to Mother Earth. I often invoked the Virgin Mary for the blessing of the earth and for humankind. My love of La Milagrosa would eventually lead me to explore other representations of Goddess from other traditions.

My psychic abilities allowed me to see spirits in between this reality and the next. I have no doubt that growing up in a family of Freemasons helped me discover more of my spiritual gifts. My mother has always been a natural psychic, having accurate premonitions that foretell things to come. She also has the gift of seeing beyond the veil, into the spirit world. I witnessed these abilities from an early age. Even when she was ill, the sight did not leave her.

ALIDA'S EXCEPTIONAL PSYCHIC GIFTS

In 2008, my mom was diagnosed with monoclonal gamapathy, a rare blood disorder that impedes the growth of red blood cells (thus hindering the body's immune response). She weighed only 98 pounds at that time, and I was fearful that I would lose her. During that time of rehabilitation, she moved to a facility where she enjoyed a beautiful suite that faced a panoramic view of Manhattan. One day, Virginia, a colleague of mine, and I came over to help Mom wash her hair. Virginia noticed that my mother did not have a hairdryer, as I recall, and we were discussing that when suddenly Mom said to me that I had to translate to Virginia what she was about to tell me. Mom said that earlier a lady had come through the terrace doors of her bedroom. I responded, "What are you talking about?" Alida said that this woman was of medium height and full figured, had salt-and-pepper hair, and wore glasses. I said, "Mom, that is simply not possible. No one can come through those terrace doors. We are sixteen flights up." My mom was not phased in the least by my logic. Instead, she continued with her story, stating that the woman on the terrace declared that Alida would get better, and that this illness was something that needed to happen during this time of her life. (This proved to be true, because Mom later went into remission.)

With sadness, I saw depression in my dear mother, and the toll of what the infections had done to her body. Her aura was very thin. To me, she was fading. My heart ached; I was very apprehensive that she might leave me so early. I didn't take her story seriously.

I then honored my mother's wish that I translate this supernatural encounter with Virginia. Virginia was not sure what to think about that story. So, we just proceeded with what needed to be done. We got Alida her dinner. We then washed her hair. Afterward, Virginia decided to go next door to borrow a hairdryer. Virginia explained to the neighbor a little of what was going on with Alida, with the request for the use of a hairdryer so that she would not get worse from the cold that comes from wet hair. The neighbor said that she agreed to lend out her hairdryer. But what she said next proved to be quite extraordinary. The neighbor said to Virginia, "I hope that she's all right. You see," the neighbor continued, "the previous tenant died on the terrace. She had suffered from a stroke. Those who came for her body had to use my terrace to jump to her terrace to retrieve her body." Stunned by this remark, given what Alida had mentioned earlier, Virginia asked for a description of that tenant. The neighbor said, "She had salt-and-pepper hair. I remember that she wore glasses. She had a dark complexion and was about medium height and on the heavy side." Virginia's hair stood on end!

At this point, I was taking care of Mom, giving her some of the food we got her. Virginia came in and nervously said that she had to tell me something. I was in awe of what Virginia had said about her conversation with the neighbor. Despite her illness, Alida had truly encountered a spirit from beyond who provided her with knowledge that she would get better. And indeed, she did! She has been in remission for over ten years now, and I am grateful.

In addition to inheriting some of my mother's natural gifts, I also learned some helpful magick from my paternal grandmother. I grew up with my grandmother's knowledge of herbalism being passed on to me. She was the equivalent of a hedge witch, I'd estimate. She used to say, "La brujería está en la mente," that translates to "Witchcraft resides in the mind." She also used to say that it is all about intent. This agrees with ancient Hermetic philosophy. Grandmother also had a famous prorverb: "Mejor que tu la tierra que pisas y después te entierran," which translates as: "Better than you is the earth you walk on, and then you are buried in it." Humility is a benchmark of maturity in witchcraft, I learned at an early age.

MY FIRST ALTAR

As far back as I can remember, my quest for spirituality was prevalent in my life, from my very tender years onward. As a child, I longed for a sacred space to honor the spirits I felt, especially during moments when premonitions and what they'd call spectral visions were particularly intense. At home, my mother's emphasis on aesthetics made any shrine or altar in my room off-limits. She had her own minimalist setup dedicated to female divinity, considering an altar an eyesore. However, my grandparents' home provided me with the spiritual freedom I sought. They recognized my old soul, always yearning for answers, and continually encouraged my spiritual development.

I was a curious and explorative boy, and one day I stumbled upon a space in my grandparents' foyer coat closet that seemed tailor-made for me. It had an inner cove deep enough to accommodate a small table, allowing me to create a shrine to angelic forces and ancestral spirits. At just about eleven years old, I found myself delving into my core being, exploring and touching my past lives, and striving to honor my ancestors.

My upbringing in Catholic mysticism instilled a love for collecting mass or holy cards of different saints; hence my fascination with "saint magick." These cards adorned the walls of my makeshift shrine in the closet, representing my interpretation of spirituality. A glass of water symbolized spirit, alongside images of my guardian angel.

Painting inspired by my first altar story, by Ernesto Pedroso

Admittedly, candles were absent. However, armed with a flashlight, I found solace in meditating with a dim glow. As an only child, I had ample time to explore concepts such as awakening the third eye, the one used for perceiving spirits and remote viewing. I emulated the rituals of my elders as closely as I could, seeking answers within the framework of Catholic thought and practice that I was steeped in. In many ways, I was self-taught, driven by the quest for the true meaning of earthly life and paving the path for spiritual guides who would soon reveal themselves.

Among the angelic forces, I embraced Michael the Archangel, a figure not formally a saint, but canonized as one by the church. He was revered as the "Prince of All Angels" and defender of the church. In my childhood, I encountered a ritual involving St. Michael, a spoken prayer combined with certain materials, a typical ritual practice. I employed it to remove unjust obstacles that might endanger my path, both as a child and later as an adult. This ritual, if memory serves, was called "The Revocation of Michael the Archangel," requiring a glass of water, a piece of paper, a white candle, and a white plate.

The ritual involved placing the focus of my intent, a person's name, for instance, on brown paper (commonly a paper grocery sack or parchment) laid on a plate. I then placed the glass of water over the paper and plate, tightly sealing it before carefully flipping it upside down. This was done where I conducted my practices because the subsequent step involved reciting the novena without interruption. During the novena, I concentrated on directing my intent, feeling a strong sense of justice and empowerment as I called upon Michael. Filled with emotion and passion, my mind and heart defied the odds, often yielding the desired results perceptibly.

SOME OF MY EARLY PARANORMAL EXPERIENCES

As a child, I had visions at the foot of my bed. There was always someone who would come and visit me from the spirit world. When this would happen, I would scream, "Mommy, mommy! Monster, monster!" Mom would try to console me by holding me and declaring that no one was there. I would see some manifestations, and I would have revelations that sometimes corresponded to my mother's premonitions, so I knew these experiences weren't "nothing."

In my childhood, I lived near a cemetery, which proved to be a contributor to my paranormal experiences. When I was in fifth grade, it was hard for me to go to school. I would go into episodes where my hands would get numb, my ears would get clogged, and I would hear the teacher far away. Then, I would hear a cackle, followed by the sound of someone trying to communicate with me; what I heard sounded very much like an old tape recording that was being played in slow motion. (The spirit could not communicate with me properly, because it was trying to do so at the wrong frequency, I later realized.) As a child, I was like a sponge. I would absorb the negative energies whenever I encountered them. I was too premature to process what was happening, and I was unaware that I needed to cleanse myself when such occurrences happened.

During the episodes, I would try to compose myself. I did not tell anyone, not even my mother. But, one day, I felt comfortable sharing my experiences with my grandmother. And she told me I was possessed. She cleansed me to her best ability. While I heard the sounds, she laid me down and placed her hands upon me and called upon our ancestors to cleanse me of the influence, reciting an old novena. Then she foretold that I would seek my own path of cleansing later on in life. I did, indeed, do my own seeking for a more permanent set of solutions in time.

I experienced a lot of spiritual activity at home on a regular basis. There were some special occasions when séances were held at home. There was a time when a group of people were there. I was still a little boy, and I remember that the door of the house was ajar. I recall having heard three knocks on the door. In response to the knocks, my grandfather said, "If you are for good, come in. If for bad, stay away." Then the door swung open. No one was visible there!

I recall having a profound, witchy experience as a child on Halloween. I was trick-or-treating on our main avenue with my mom. I walked alongside her as she pushed my one-year-old cousin in her carriage. I wore a mask from the legendary Woolworth's, as I recall. This mask made it difficult for me to see that a cellar door on the ground was open, and I fell through! On my way down, I had a spiritual experience. I lost consciousness for a mere second, and I found myself at a willow tree, playing with a yellow ball. It was peaceful and heavenly! I could feel a calmness that made me feel that the tree was some sort of portal. I also heard voices in the distance, seeming to come from behind the tree, which sparked my curiosity. This whole experience happened in a second or two, while I was rolling down those cellar stairs. When I came to, one of the nearby workers caught me, stopping my fall. I was immediately given back to my mom. Amazingly, I didn't even have a bruise on my body.

As an adult, I later understood that the willow tree has always been known as the tree of dreaming and enchantment. It is also known as the tree of immortality because of its ability to regrow from a fallen branch in moist ground. It is associated in Celtic legend with poets and with spells of fascination. It possesses a particular energy that puts us in touch with our feelings and deep emotions. Our deep subconscious mind, associated with our soul, speaks to us through our dreams. Having a willow wand and sleeping with it always enhances our dreams, since it makes our dreams more vivid and meaningful. The willow tree is the source of one of our most common drugs, acetylsalicylic acid, known commonly as aspirin. Infusions from the bark have long been used for treating colds, rheumatism, and fevers.

Along with its medicinal properties, I use willow for its lunar magick, specifically new-moon magick, for drawing or strengthening love, healing, and overcoming sadness. The willow's energy also inspires us with creativity. Witches can use them for besoms or other ritual tools. Willow is considered sacred by many, and it is a powerful wishing tree. If you wear a sprig of willow when facing the death of a loved one, the willow helps calm you. Place it on your altar on a full moon for divination or protection from visitors with unwanted energies that might come to do you harm. I also came to realize that this magickal tree helps us with easing our transition into the Summerland, which may be why I had the experience with the willow tree at Samhain. This may explain the out-of-body experience and the voices I heard coming from behind the tree in my vision.

Freemasonry is "veiled in allegory and illustrated by symbols" because these are the surest way by which moral and ethical truths may be taught. It is not only with the brain and with the mind that the initiate must take Freemasonry but also with the heart.

—C. H. Claudy

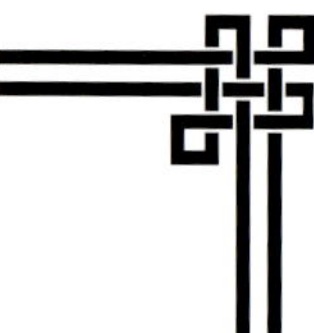

CHAPTER 1
FREEMASONRY

I first entered the Masonic Lodge's doors at a tender age. My mother would lead me in by the hand. Even though I was young, I could sense that Freemasonry was a magickal order. The magickal energy was in everything: the symbols, the people, the uniforms, the rituals. It was even in the air. I could feel the ancient history, the spiritual fervor, and the raw power of the order. For me, there was no mistaking the magickal energy; it was truly palpable!

A RICH BUT TUMULTUOUS HISTORY

Freemasonry, as it exists today, comes from the previous order of the Knights Templar. The Knights Templar were a group of wealthy and well-armed men with architectural knowledge and an insatiable thirst for learning more about Solomon's Temple and, their ultimate goal, to learn the whereabouts of the Ark of the Covenant (their secret "grail" quest) and to recover it. They were originally called the Poor Fellow-Soldiers of Christ and of the Temple of Solomon, and several shorter nicknames ensued, and we are left with the popular "Templars" or "Knights Templar."

Quite some time after being founded, and after occupying the temple mound at Jerusalem while searching for the ark, they were able to garner the support of a cardinal and subsequently were sanctioned by the Catholic Church as an official Holy Order. Later, their mission to recover the Ark of the Covenant for themselves was likely discovered by the church, who quickly reversed their support. A subsequent huge sting operation was carried out on the secret commission of an enraged Pope Clement V to try to arrest, interrogate, and even kill them and seize their belongings. The order seemed all but wiped out, especially in France and England. Afterward, the surviving members disguised themselves, sometimes forming new organizations. Many became known as Freemasons. The Order of Christ, in Portugal, was another incarnation of the Templars. They built a notably large and sturdy fortress for themselves there. There were many, all over the globe, but in what is now the United Kingdom, the modern order of Free and Accepted Masons got its start under that name. The secretive order is known to have once again spread from Europe to the Caribbean and the Americas via the Age of Exploration during the Renaissance time period, and there is also evidence that the previous Templars had spread globally much earlier than that period, to Egypt and even Ethiopia and the North American continent. They amassed a great deal of esoteric knowledge in their explorations, under any banner during their history. Their rites were and are deeply full of meaningful symbolism, with powerful spiritual energy. No wonder I felt it so deeply.

SECRETS AND SKILLS

Because of the tragic end so many Templars faced at the hands of what was arguably the most influential organization in the history of the world, it is easy to understand that from its earliest times it has been a secretive society. The passwords and secret rites of Freemasons, the secret hand grips and phrases, and the method of inducting new members by being vetted and then sponsored by existing members all added up to necessary security to avoid another tragedy that could threaten their existence. They (or their predecessors the Templars) were responsible for building or supplying the plans for the most-breathtaking cathedrals in the world, many of which still stand today. Fortunately, even though the Catholic Church still strongly discourages any of their followers to become a part of the order(s), the threat of extermination is greatly lessened in our modern day, and the Free and Accepted Masons are a lot more open. If you suspect someone is a Mason, all you need to do is ask, and they will answer honestly. To become a Mason, one need only ask an existing one how to go about joining, and already the journey toward the "light" will have begun.

The UK-area guilds met in lodges in both Scotland and England, but some of the earliest records point to Edinburgh, Scotland, in the 1500s as the possible birthplace and birth time period of what we may call modern Freemasonry. A matter of debate, but we still find at least some of the oldest lodges in those areas.

As Masonry was designed and evolved, they encoded sacred geometry and alchemical knowledge into their tools and symbols of architecture and masonry, calling God the Grand Architect. Sayings such as "on the level" and "fair and square" come from Freemasonry. Sacred writings, such as the Bible, are often there to direct their faith, but for most lodges the only religious requirement for new members is monotheism and creation belief.

JOURNEY INTO THE LIGHT

Every Freemason's journey originates from a state of (figurative) darkness. It is the job of the initiate to embark on a path toward the light. As they progress to further initiations, they are said to seek "more light" from the East. Initiation is a test, a work to be done, and also a rite of passage. There are three degrees in their system of progression; namely, Entered Apprentice, Fellowcraft (also called Journeyman or Mason), and Master Mason. The highest-level Freemason is called a Master Mason, and although there are a few additional degrees that may be conferred upon them, those are supplementary or specialty degrees rather than higher degrees, for there are none higher than Master Mason. "The Master Mason is then invested with different offices each year, acting out different parts of the ritual until he becomes the Worshipful Master of his lodge. He will sit in the 'Chair' and direct and rule his lodge for the ensuing year, after which he will become a Worshipful Brother and have a distinctly designed regalia" (courtesy of Christopher White, a Master Mason and Worshipful Brother of Northern England). There are offshoot organizations and alternative fraternities of similar origin that have varying other degrees, such as the famous 33rd degree of the Scottish Rite. Only the three levels mentioned above are meaningful to the actual Freemasons, though.

At its core, it stands for brotherhood and maintaining morality, for building civilization with civil principles, and for emulating God, the Grand Architect. This is the oath that all Freemasons have taken, according to some sources:

> *These points I solemnly swear to observe under no less penalty than to have my throat cut across, my tongue torn out by the root and buried at low water mark where the tide ebbs and flows.*

MASONS BUILDING THE WORLD

There have been many influential members of this society all over the world. They have built countries along with buildings. There have been many United States presidents who are said to have taken the above oath, including (but not limited to) George Washington, Andrew Jackson, Franklin D. Roosevelt, and Harry S. Truman.

The well-known American silversmith, engraver, and industrialist Paul Revere was the Worshipful Master (head of the lodge) in Boston at the time of the famous Boston Tea Party event. Other familiar Freemasons were John Hancock and Benjamin Franklin, both signers of the United States Declaration of Independence. In fact, the idea of freedom and equality of all under a creator, found in the Declaration of Independence, existed within the tenets of Freemasonry. It is true that Freemasons are said to be the guardians of democracy and the backbone of American history. A cursory study of their history will reveal that they have been present and working at the founding or the evolution of many other countries as well.

FREEMASONS IN CUBA

Freemasonry was first brought to Cuba under "tragic" conditions, due to the "Negro revolution in Haiti" circa 1793 to 1810. The Grand Lodge of Pennsylvania was chartered in Havana on December 17, 1804 (Le Temple des Vertus Theogales, number 103), with Joseph Cerneau as first Master. Three lodges originally constituted in Haiti were reorganized at Santiago de Cuba in 1805–1806.

> Masonry has been an active force in the growth of democracy in Cuba. . . . The Ten Years War (1868–1878) was inspired and waged by patriots—many of whom were Freemasons—who helped frame the Constitution of Guaimaro (1869), a genuinely democratic document.
>
> — Warren H. Murphy, "A History of Freemasonry in Cuba," *Walter F. Meier Lodge of Research* 281

The history of the lodges in Cuba was turbulent, according to "A History of Freemasonry in Cuba," an address published in 1968 and written by Warren H. Murphy, P.M., who was a former Master of Maritime

Lodge (no. 239). Despite lodge closings (due to inactivity) and reorganizing from time to time, and various troubles with establishments, Freemasonry became a staple of Cuban society. It certainly had a profound effect on the men of my lineage, who had long been a part of that "active force in the growth of democracy." "In 2010, it was reported that the island [of Cuba] had 316 Masonic lodges, and more than 29,000 active members" (retrieved on March 28, 2021, from https://www.exutopia.com/fidel-castro-the-curious-case-of-freemasonry-in-cuba).

When Castro took power in 1959, the official Masons closed shop and moved to Florida, while he took over all of their lodges in Cuba, seized all records and property therein, and took charge of their activities. He was able to garner the support and permission of a lodge in Florida, at first, to become the new Master of Masons in Cuba. A year later, having denied his "brothers" liberties and considerations, the Masonic Lodge in Florida officially cut any and all ties with him. Any remaining true Freemasons met and worked only in secret while he was in power. Masons from Cuba from then on had to bear special credentials proving they were "real" Masons, rather than those from Castro's regime version of Masonry.

Freemasonry symbol atop the Grand Lodge of Havana, Cuba

OUR FAMILY CONTINUES THE TRADITION

Fast forward to the 1970s: My parents, Alida and Salvador, chose a local lodge (in West New York, New Jersey) that was convenient for our family to attend. I felt the energy from the doors of the great hall. I have many memories of being involved with the adults for congregated celebratory events in that room. I was in awe of the solemn feeling of secrecy that hummed in the walls and lit through the air. (Obviously, none of the private ceremonies were ever shown to me at that young age, but I could still sense the powerful energy from them.)

As a child, I was thrilled to visit the lodge to play with my friends. There was an enclosed room designated for children. This room was supervised by a pretty young lady, as I recall. We could be free to enjoy wonderful playtimes, full of fantasy and wonder, while our parents busied themselves with their activities in private. I was delighted with the many friendships forged in those walls, and the occasional experiences I had physically and spiritually there.

I was deeply moved by the remarkable transformation of my mother during this time. Due to my father's influence, she decided to become initiated in the Order of the Eastern Star. After her initiation, her aura glowed brighter and there was a noticeable presence of power that she did not exhibit prior to that. It thrilled me to see her like that! Afterward, I was filled with peace when I witnessed both of my parents, further bonded by their involvement in the secret orders, during their quiet reflections.

During my own quiet time, I would reflect on the spiritual legacies of the men in my family. Aside from the Freemasonry Order, I was aware of a great-grandfather, Ismael de la Rue, who was an alchemist and occultist. He would serve as a very influential role model for me.

Ismael de la Rue, my great-grandfather, Havana, Cuba, 1914

MASONIC SYMBOLS

One symbol that my heart grew to revere was the pentagram. The first time I had noticed it was at the Masonic temple, rather than in a witchcraft-related setting. Later, I saw it at home as well. In Freemasonry, the pentagram is a symbol full of many secret meanings that the initiates learn. There are two meanings of the pentagram that have been revealed to the public, however. One is that it represents the elements. The other is that it is the "Blazing Star," which some say relates to the star Sirius (other sources claim that it refers to Venus). The pentagram, in its upright and inverted forms, is used during Freemasons' ceremonies.

Another symbol that I was enamored with was the Eye of Providence. It is often depicted in Freemasonry within a triangle or pyramid shape. One day, during a casual conversation with one of the elders, he informed me that the Eye of Providence pertains to the All (Source energy within the All).

REGALIA

As a kid with a natural talent for aesthetic visuals, I knew and appreciated the fashion sense of the many who came into the lodge dressed to the hilt. My mother was certainly one of them. I admired the way she was dressed in such grace and elegance, with her fancy scarf and her suit jacket, which reflected that time period. Dressing in specific attire was important when performing magickal ceremonies in the temple. At my age, I didn't notice the variances by office or rank, but I always admired the finery.

The Mother Goddess was guiding me toward the Path of the Old Religion via my childhood experiences in Freemasonry. While in the lodge visiting my friends,

I felt that I was, by the Mother Goddess's help, able to somehow recharge or reattune my mystical energies. (This was something I felt but could not explain in words then.)

MUCH MORE THAN CATHOLIC

I understood that my parents were not ordinary folks following the mainstream, accepted Christian path. My family came from a long line of freethinkers. I often pondered this fact as I was sent to Sunday school and Sunday Mass (as, it seemed, every young Catholic Cuban American boy was). Outwardly, Cuban Americans in our community all seemed to be Catholic, but there was always a greater depth and an air of secrecy under the surface.

It was certainly a challenge for me, as a young boy, to balance the dogmatic religious structure of Catholicism with my family's mystical and occult legacies. It seemed to me that my mind was able to pick up higher frequencies than my strictly Catholic classmates. Perhaps it was a higher-frequency awareness, higher consciousness, that allowed me to psychically process the spiritual realm that lay outside the confines of Catholic explanation. It was this perceptive ability and the underlying calling that paved the way for me to develop into the man I am today.

Mejor que tu la tierra que pisas y después te entierran. [Better than you is the earth you walk on; and then you are buried in it.]

—My grandmother Gloria Batistapau

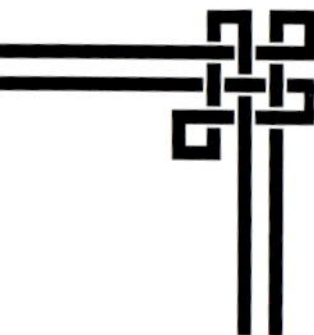

CHAPTER 2
RENAISSANCE OCCULTISM

The Middle Ages were filled with the power of the Catholic Church, but in the midst of the religion, there were those who practiced Christian mysticism. It was tolerated by the church, because certain saints were known mystics (including St. Columba, famous for having said, "Jesus is my Druid"), and because some (more likely many) of their cardinals were practitioners of High Ritual Magick. It was due to the Catholic monks that mysticism lived on in Celtic Christianity. Many of the Pagan converts (including the Druids) to Catholicism practiced their magick through the "new" Catholic mysticism. (Instead of bedtime stories, my grandparents told me stories regarding mysticism in Christianity. It was fascinating! I was young enough to absorb and dissect this without mental blocks.)

Later, anything mystical (magickal/occult) was proclaimed to be evil by the church. The magickal arts are very clerical in nature, and even knowledge and learning, reading and basic sciences, were discouraged for the common people during these dark times. The church spoon fed the people what they wanted them to think religiously, setting themselves even more deeply as the only outlet for God's will and the mouthpiece of the divine. Assuming the role of the only legitimate teachers or guides, they succeeded in cementing their position of power over the people. Heresy (literally, "free thinking") was anything that didn't come from them or agree with them, and it was often punishable by death. Many people (magickal and nonmagickal practitioners alike) were persecuted and even sometimes killed for practicing "the dark arts." At the same time, many of the cardinals and bishops of the church were still practitioners of ceremonial magick themselves. As with other learning, they wanted to monopolize this knowledge and the resulting power.

This continues, in some measure, through today in many areas around the world, especially some areas of the African continent. Magickal practitioners were (and sometimes still are) forced into hiding in order to save themselves and their loved ones from harm. In my own way, even here in the "land of the free" in our modern age, I also sometimes felt like I had to hide my magickal side due to society's judgments. I was told to keep careful discretion, even to keep my magick occult, meaning "in hiding" or "in darkness." All it takes is one misguided zealot to end a life.

My grandparents and I, Union City, New Jersey, 1975

THE RENAISSANCE

However, the heavy European persecution abated, for the most part, with the dawn of the Renaissance. The word "Renaissance" translates to "new birth" or "rebirth." (The word "renaissance" means a lot to me, because in my view it is about empowerment and spiritual alchemy, the transmutation of the spirit, initiation, growth, and needed change.) There was a massive new birth, a transformation in people's lives. This was the time when the sciences (not religion) became prominent in the culture of Italy (the birthplace of the Renaissance time period). Scientific disciplines that prospered during that time were primarily astronomy, physics, and mathematics.

For our purposes, we will look at the occult sciences from the Renaissance. These primarily originated from ancient Hermetic teachings by Hermes Trismegistus, as recounted in the Corpus Hermeticum, or "Hermetic Body." The most prominent and influential of the sayings in Hermeticism is "As Above, So Below." That is a basic principle of magick, and a foundational one, no matter what system is involved.

One of the strongest and most influential scientists of the Renaissance was Sir Isaac Newton. Schools today teach that he discovered the scientific force of gravity, and there are numerous other scientific discoveries attributed to him, such as his work on the laws of motion. However, what most postmodern students fail to realize is that Newton was an avid believer in Hermeticism. This inspired him to practice magick via the occult sciences of astrology and alchemy. Those things are what actually lit his inner fire for physics. My grandparents' teachings of occultism helped ground me, and when I studied about Newton in my classes, I felt a strong connection with him. As a practitioner in his day, he blended science and mysticism. He inspired me to also balance science with mysticism, keeping an open-eyed pragmatism with the traditional teachings.

Astrology (the study of how the cosmos affects us here on Earth) was brought to the West via interactions with the Middle East, especially Persia (modern-day Iran). The origins of astrology itself take us back into murky historical waters, perhaps prehistory, but we at least trace the oldest known system for detailed horoscopes to ancient Babylon. There is a legend that, after the great flood, there was a stela found with the details of astrology as they had been passed to humans from fallen angels. Some attribute it instead to Seth, a son of Adam, but no matter how old, we are pretty sure it came from Persia to the West. Those familiar with the nativity story of Jesus Christ know of the "wise men" (astrologers and advisors to King Herod) who came from the East. These were most likely sages/magicians from Persia. Arabian neighbors of Persia also learned the occult sciences, including astrology, from Persian sages in most cases.

ARTHURIAN LEGEND AND THE ORIGINS OF ESOTERIC MIGRATION WESTWARD

According to Professor Roland Rotherham, whom I met in Tintagel, England, Merlin was most likely an Arabian or Persian sage, who brought the occult sciences to the West with him. However, according to Arthur Uther Pendragon, also of England, the story of Merlin has been told as a result of the Christianization of history. It is my personal suspicion that the Knights Templar may have sometimes been responsible for bringing information on ancient, Middle Eastern magick on their missions to western Europe. Over the years, I have always been fascinated with Knights Templar lore and was excited by the idea of their probable association with ancient Persian sages and mystics. What did they pick up from the Middle East while headquartered in Jerusalem? Yes, I tend to suspect it was through them that some of the science and magick of astrology came to the West, at least in recognizable historical terms. I also recognize that monks and missionaries from the Catholic Church often were responsible for documenting esoteric information, but most of the time that sort of thing was kept hidden from outsiders.

ENOCHIAN LANGUAGE AND MINDSET

Doctor John Dee, Queen Elizabeth I's court astrologer, was one who practiced science and mysticism. Well trained in the disciplines of mathematics, astronomy, and navigation, he was also a well-known and respected Renaissance man for his extraordinary work with the development (or discovery) of Enochian language and magick. My grandparents informed me in my youth that Enochian is the language of angels. According to the story, it was angels who visited John Dee. He claimed that they dictated their language to him. The belief was that it is from this language that we can connect with the angels in a profound way, by meeting them on "their terms." Angelic and saint magick was very much a part of my grandparents' personal practice (they understood this practice to be part of Christian mysticism). My grandparents enjoyed working specifically with St. Michael, the archangel, who was placed by the front door to protect the household. (For more on Enochian language development, history, and practice, see the next chapter's article on Crowley by Aron Paramor.)

ASTROLOGY

Over time, astrology made its way from western Europe to the Caribbean. In my youth, I was fascinated by astrology due to the influence of Walter Mercado. Mercado was a famous Puerto Rican astrologer, medium, and mystic that came into my community in the 1970s. We called him the Liberace of Astrology because he was very flamboyant. There were many who criticized him for being androgynous. Nonetheless, he was Hispanic, so he was accepted as part of the community, "one of us." As a child, I fondly remember how families in our community would gather around our television sets to watch Mercado's TV show. From my perspective, I remember the children loving to be entertained by Mercado as he provided that day's horoscope report. We could not help but to be captivated by his exceptional, loving energy that would transmit to us via our TVs. I smile as I remember that Mercado would say, "Let there be peace and harmony. Lots and lots and lots of love!"

ALCHEMY AND THE PHILOSOPHER'S STONE

The next part of Renaissance occultism I wish to discuss is alchemy (something very dear to me). When today's young adults think about alchemy, there is undoubtedly a connection to the philosopher's or sorcerer's stone, fashioned by the famous alchemist Nicholas Flamel. Reputedly, Nicholas Flamel was able to live a long life due to his success in making the aforementioned stone, for this stone, by its alchemical properties, was said to help a person live forever. In truth, the "stone" is symbolic of the basic building material of the universe, a substance from which it was believed anything else could be made (called in Latin the *prima materia*, or first material). Breaking matter down to its simplest part and then creating other matter from it was the basis of the physical representation of the Great Work, which more often referred to a process of remaking ourselves for spiritual enlightenment and progress. The longevity or healing effects they hoped for were tied to the idea of how we now see stem cells—something that can become anything that is needed. Indeed, cellular dedifferentiation and redifferentiation is the key to regeneration. In our bodies, certain types of cells revert to a more basic cellular form, a nonspecific one, then become what is needed. That is essentially how broken bones are able to mend, for instance, since cells simplify and become nonspecific, then form cartilage, which then further changes into bone.

Next to Flamel, Paracelsus was a highly influential alchemist. He is recorded to have formulated that alchemical elements were, at their core, boiled down to the four elements: water, earth, fire, and air. Undines (a word he used to refer to water spirits) existed within the water element. Gnomes lived in and influenced the earth element. Salamanders were associated with the fire element. Sylphs were the inhabitants of the air element. Paracelsus used what he had learned about alchemy to create chemical formulae to cure diseases. This was the basis of an understanding of chemistry, and it was to be one of the starting points of modern-day chemical medicine. The desire to reduce matter to its base components in order to better understand it and work with it led to our current periodic table. Likely, it was influenced also by Chinese medicine, which involved "hot" and "cold" varieties of medicine and associated their five elements with various medicines and ailments. Ayurvedic medicine from India predated it as well and may have held some of its roots.

Of course, medicine back then and also in today's world need not pertain only to physical ailments. It also can relate to spiritual maladies. Today, alchemy is still practiced in the form of spiritual ascent (something that I practice regularly). Reducing ourselves to our base makeup and renewing our existence, a rebirth, as it were, is a basic component of many spiritual practices, and it is alchemy at its core. As a practicing witch, I use spiritual alchemy to help my spirit continue to grow, to ascend to higher levels of awareness. Some look to the ancient Greek goddess Sophia (Goddess of Wisdom) to help them master spiritual alchemy. However, I invoke Goddess and my guides to help me with my alchemical workings.

Rudolf Steiner wrote about the Greek goddess Sophia in his book *The Goddess: From Natura to Divine Sophia*. Other notable references to Sophia as relating to a wisdom goddess can be seen in Helena Blavatsky's essay titled "What Is Theosophy?" Also, Sophia is recognized as one of the manifestations of the Goddess of Wisdom in Sorita d'Este's *The Cosmic Shekinah*. It is thought that Goddess Sophia of the Greeks is the same Wisdom whom King Solomon (of the Israelites) referred to. According to some, it was Wisdom's magical teachings that gave Solomon his power over demons. The Seal of Solomon is said to protect one from evil forces. Many occultists of the Renaissance used this seal along with nonbiblical magical spells in Solomonic Magic. I fondly remember that, when I was eleven years of age, I used the Seal of Solomon in one of my first magical workings.

NOSTRADAMUS

The history of Renaissance occultism is not complete without mentioning the famous Nostradamus. Michel de Nostredame was born on December 14, 1503, in St. Remy de Provence, France. His parents were Jewish, but they decided to convert to Catholicism. As a young child, Michel believed his visions came from God, but he did not have any idea what to do with the gift of prophecy that he possessed.

My grandparents taught me much about Nostradamus when I was a child. I remember being with them at home when they would tell me about Nostradamus's legacy. My grandmother enjoyed telling me about specific prophecies. When she would do so, she wore a floral apron while baking her delicious bread pudding and bunt cakes. While I was in the kitchen, helping Grandmother with her baking, my grandfather was in the parlor, wearing his smoking jacket and smoking his Cuban cigar (illegal to import to the USA directly, so friends of the family would send them to him from Madrid, Spain), and reading his Spanish edition of the *Reader's Digest*. Grandfather read occult science literature as well. I recall him telling me about Tibetan Buddhists levitating. It is common knowledge that Tibetan Buddhists have gone through hardship brought by China, including the displacement of the Dalai Lama, but it is not as commonly known that Tibetan Buddhists practice occult magick. Periodically, he would come into the kitchen to chime in with the conversation on Nostradamus or the occult (or both).

My grandparents taught me that Nostradamus learned the stories of the Bible, including the prophetic stories, which he undoubtedly connected to due to his gift of prophecy. While growing up, Michel studied the teachings of Kabbalah, astrology, Latin, and Greek, among other things. (As an awakened spiritual being, I also felt the need to study various paths of magick. One such path is Kabbalah. Like alchemy, Kabbalah helps with one's spiritual growth as one stays connected, centered on Source.) When he was older, he changed his name to Nostradamus, and he studied medicine. My grandparents taught me that Nostradamus changed his name due to the persecution of the Jews in that time period. There is a great article titled "Saturn and the Jews" that details some of the reasons why Jews were persecuted during the Renaissance. Nostradamus became very popular for his peculiar healing methods, which strayed from contemporaneous medicine. Nostradamus refused to bleed patients, even though standard medicine used this method to rid the body of impurities/infection. Instead, my grandparents told me that Nostradamus invented a rose lozenge, filled with vitamin C, that helped prevent people from getting the plague and that helped heal plague victims.

After his first wife and two kids died of the plague, Nostradamus led a nomadic life, moving from town to town. There was a part of him that must have doubted his healing abilities, due to the demise of his beloved family members. This heavy heart likely led him to study the occult much more closely.

Nostradamus learned to work with his visions with his knowledge of the occult. He used a specific form of pyromancy (divination by flame gazing) and water scrying (divination by looking into water, as if by looking into a

Gloria and Cristobal, my grandparents, Havana, Cuba, 1964

mirror) and a wand. Specifically, my grandparents told me that he used black ink in water. Scryers often use black mirrors to this day. While doing these things, he saw amazing visions that he would later pen down, with an accuracy that has inspired wonder in readers ever since.

He wrote around one thousand prophecies in a cryptic fashion. He wrote them in various languages, including Latin and Greek. He wrote them in poetic fashion, all in rhyming quatrains. Much to the dismay of scholars, his many prophecies were completely out of chronological order. My grandmother was extremely passionate about Nostradamus. I grew up hearing about his prophecies and how some of them were believed to have come to pass in the twentieth century, including Hitler's Nazi regime and World War II.

From the twentieth century came the reawakening of many. Druids and witches and other occultists came out of hiding. Many of us were free to practice our magick much like those of the Renaissance, and it is my desire to reveal what I have learned and practiced in order to help other magickal beings on their spiritual journeys. By no means do I offer a how-to manual here, since it takes a long time of dedicated and well-guided practice to gain the skills needed, but this is a chronicle of my journey, offered in the hope of inspiring the journeys of others.

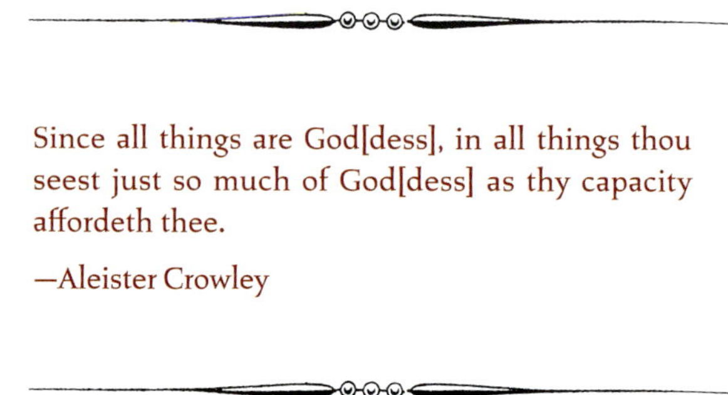

Since all things are God[dess], in all things thou seest just so much of God[dess] as thy capacity affordeth thee.

—Aleister Crowley

CHAPTER 3
ALEISTER CROWLEY

One of the most inspirational people to me when growing up was Aleister Crowley. I first learned about him at the age of eleven. He was undeniably the most influential occult figure of the twentieth century, and I found out about this magnificent occultist from such works as *Moon Child*, *The Qabbalah of Aleister Crowley*, and *Book of the Law*.

Crowley still inspires me. As I write this chapter, I do so having just been visited by him in my dreams. In those dreams, he has given me his blessing to honor him in my memoirs. He has shown me the path to the Golden Dawn. His message for us is that magick exists within us all; our existence flows with magick. His presence is tangible to me and will undoubtedly be profound for readers as well.

My favorite book by Crowley is *Moon Child*. In it, I learned that men could and should revere female divinity. I am grateful to Crowley because the magick of the Goddess was revealed as real energy, consciousness, and universal power. We can, via the Goddess, manipulate that energy with intention. It is our birthright, and She is our mother from which we get our existence and sustenance.

One of my first glimpses into the ancient Hermetic teachings stems from my reading of Crowley's *Book of the Law*. Crowley's teachings were based on the freethinking, magickal philosophies of the ancient Greeks. Thelema was the core of Crowley's theology. The word "thelema" is the Greek word for "will."

Crowley's Thelema is as follows: "Do what thou wilt shall be the whole of the law. Love is the law, love under will." That statement inspired many, such as Doreen Valiente, and it inspired me too. As an eleven-year-old youngster, my interpretation of Crowley's Thelema was that it was all about the higher consciousness. To me, it also taught that every person's awareness has always been with them, and it will be with them after their physical existence on this planet.

I found Crowley's writings to be mind-blowing. Although a young boy, I had the wisdom to hide Crowley's works, along with copies of *Man, Myth, and Magic* and the *Encyclopedia of Witchcraft*, along with whatever I could check out from the library, in my closet (I was literally a closet witch). I knew my parents were outwardly Catholic and inwardly freethinkers of Freemasonry, but I feared that since English was not their first language, they would not have the knowledge to read and to grasp the meaning of Crowley's works. They would have probably forbidden the reading of those texts to protect me.

There existed no anonymity with Crowley—he was no closet witch. I found that fascinating! So many occultists and other magickal practitioners were not so open about their practices back then. (This highly differs from the plethora of magickal practitioners who are currently practicing their workings publicly via social media.) Crowley was bold; he was definitely not mainstream. There were many who called him 666, the mark of the beast, and he was proud of that! He loved the attention, positive or negative, and he used it to his advantage.

Later on, while I was in my thirties, I was in awe that Crowley's legacy was so grand that he was featured on the cover of *Rolling Stone* magazine. Despite the controversy associated with Crowley's life, he always had the Goddess with him. I believed it then, and I believe it still.

Aleister Crowley's life was truly one of polarity. After his father unexpectedly passed away when he was young, Crowley's grief turned to hate, and he took out that hate on his mother. The Goddess knew this, pitying him. It is my belief that She reached out to him through his love of the occult while he was attending university. It was Goddess who showed him the Order of the Golden Dawn. He grew to become a powerful magickal practitioner. However, his anger grew again. His confrontational, rebellious nature led to him getting rejected by the order.

Goddess again intervened through Crowley's wife, Rose. I believe the Goddess caused Rose to channel messages from the god Horus via a powerful spirit called Aiwass during their honeymoon in Egypt. Afterward, Crowley would write his *Book of the Law*, that which birthed Thelema, the foundation of his legacy.

As time went on, so did his magickal teachings and followers. He inspired many people to be the magickal beings they were. One of the things he taught others was the power of sex magick, a thing I didn't understand fully at eleven years of age, but later I could grasp the value of it. With ancient roots, there are Welsh Druids still practicing it today, learned from countless generations before them. While it wasn't a new concept, he certainly popularized it in his day, and there were many who decided to engage in that type of magick to strengthen their personal will and power.

However, he did go overboard, as he had in the past, again and again. Eventually, his magick turned dark. He was much like Grigori Yefimovich Rasputin (the unorthodox clergyman of the Romanoff family of Russia who was responsible for their deaths), one full of immense power and promise, who had chosen to go down a path toward the dark arts.

Despite his flaws, I still honor the good work that came from Aleister Crowley. He and his legacy still have a special place in my heart. Also, as aforementioned, I still am in awe of his boldness, to be who he was as a highly influential occultist of the twentieth century. I am honored to channel his boldness to help me write this book and share my life with my brothers and sisters of the craft today.

On a vacation in Brazil with my great friend Susan Marie Paramore, Susan remotely introduced me to her son, via an internet video chat, who is a world-class expert on Aleister Crowley. What better person to enlighten us about Aleister Crowley other than Aron Paramor, in the following article written specifically for inclusion in this work?

The devil has been described as "myth;" hence he exists and continues to be active. A myth is a story which describes and illustrates in dramatic form certain deep structures of society.

—Denis de Rougemont

I loved reading Crowley's work.

ALEISTER CROWLEY: THE MAN, THE MYTH, THE MAGICK, AND THE MESSAGE

AN ARTICLE BY ARON PARAMOR, 2021, WRITTEN AND DONATED FOR THIS WORK

The Beast, 666, Mega Therion, Wanderer of the Waste—the name of Aleister Crowley still inspires horror, ridicule, disgust, and admiration through his outrageous activities and teachings even today. The ultimate rebel of his age, he was a bisexual man with a huge sex drive, enjoying homosexual liaisons as much as heterosexual. He experimented with every drug he could lay his hands on, and he struggled with addiction. By the end of his life, he was taking single doses of heroin large enough to kill a roomful of people.

Crowley explored the unconscious, specifically through magick, studying ancient manuscripts, grimoires, and treatises, in order to synthesize and modernize them. A prolific writer, he also broke mountaineering records and traveled the world. Unknown to many, he was a chess master, painter, novelist, secret agent, and poet. His black sense of humor shocked and outraged people, encouraging an already vindictive and sensationalist press to dub him "the Wickedest Man in the World" or "the King of Depravity." More importantly, he believed himself to be a new messiah on a divine mission to spread the Law of Thelema. In Crowley's words, he was "one hell of a Holy Guru."

Born Edward Alexander Crowley, on the night of October 12, 1875, at precisely 10:50 p.m., at Clarendon Square, Leamington Spa, Warwickshire, he entered the straightjacketed world of Victorian morals, manners, and platitudes. His early religious experience was through his parents' membership in the Plymouth Brethren, a sect with a strict doctrine that rejected anything outside the Bible. Indeed, for them, the fossils we saw had been placed in the earth by the devil, who sought to trick people into disbelieving the Genesis account. Deeply loyal to his father, with only the Bible to read at first, young Crowley would join his father in preaching in the street. His preferred method was to break down a man, right to his final moment, by asking, "What are you going to do?" and then answering, again and again, "and then?" until the person was often reduced to tears, contemplating his own demise, and his already wasted life. At that point, Crowley's father would interject, "Exactly! Get right with God!" It's easy to imagine the young boy, immersed in his fanatical Bible study, echoing, "Yes, father. Get right with God."

Crowley inherited his father's fortune, made (ironically) from brewing alcohol. He was devastated by his father's death. The most important man in his life had died from tongue cancer, and Aleister turned to bitterness and contempt for all things Christian in his grief. Crowley treated his widowed mother abominably, who called him afterward "the Little Beast." Young Crowley took her words gleefully and identified himself with the beast of Revelation, identified with the mark 666. His rejection and mistreatment of his mother continued throughout his adulthood. Victor Neuburg, having had a meal with Aleister and his mother, witnessed the very active spite when he heard Aleister tell his still deeply religious mother that the food on her plate was "fried Jesuit."

After his severe "boyhood in hell," Crowley attended Cambridge College and, in his own words, "wanted to be something that nobody else had ever been or could be." He embraced his role as the enfant terrible, one of the original Angry Young Men (a group of novelists and playwrights who eventually experienced peak prominence in the 1950s). He pursued the art of poetry, writing passionate, romantic, and magickal verse. The early work of that sort can still be found collected in three volumes, published by the Yogi Publication Society. Today, several of his poems are included in mainstream anthologies, including the *Oxford Book of English Mystical Verse*. Those wishing to explore his poetry further should read Martin Booth's excellent collected anthology, *Aleister Crowley: Selected Poems*, published in 1986 by Crucible.

On November 18, 1898, Crowley was made a member of the Golden Dawn. That is the moment he answered his calling by taking the magickal name Perdurabo, meaning "I will endure." It does encapsulate the Crowley essence. The Hermetic Order of the Golden Dawn, already founded ten years earlier, dissolved into splinter factions in the next five years following Crowley's induction. An inner order was formed by Samuel Liddell MacGregor Mathers, called the Order of the Rose and the Cross of Gold, which gave instruction in ritual magick. The Golden Dawn became the crowning glory of the occult revival of the 1800s, cofounded by Mathers and two others, and its members counted the literary and poetic elite. These included but were not limited to Sir Arthur Conan Doyle, Bram Stoker, Algernon Blackwood, W. B. Yeats, Constance Lloyd (wife of Oscar Wilde), and later Dion Fortune as well. H. P. Lovecraft was even rumored to have been a part of its ranks.

Since most of the secret teachings and "flying scrolls" have now been published, it has become possible to access Crowley's foundational teachings. Those were based on Egyptian mysteries, Scottish Freemasonry rites, ritual magick, Hermeticism, alchemy, Enochian magick, astral-plane travel, study of the Tarot, numerology, geomancy, the adoption of god forms, and even invisibility. These things formed the core of the Western Magickal Tradition as we know it now. The secret grade system, from the probationer to the magus, is now accessible to the newcomer. The Golden Dawn's foundational study of the Tree of Life is the Rosetta stone of the modern magickal world and the human unconscious. Once one commits to a path of enlightenment in the declaration, saying that "with the Divine permission I will, from this day forward, apply myself to the Great Work, which is to purify and exalt my spiritual nature, that I may at length attain to be more than human and thus gradually raise and unite myself with my higher and divine genius, and in this event, I will not abuse the great powers entrusted to me," the Golden Dawn offers a clear path ahead, with signposts along the way.

The meteoric rise and fall of the Golden Dawn serves as a cautionary tale to all of us who wish to walk the occult path. Without protective rituals in place, we can overinflate our egos and fall prey to imagination, risking descent into utter madness. The infighting of clashing personalities, sexual resentments, and conflicting or ambitious desires that often sew the doom of organizations are normal occurrences within group dynamics. Working with ourselves as lone wolves is a more popular route these days, but we then risk missing out on the collective human experience, such as a Gnostic Mass. Thee Temple ov Psychick Youth was a fellowship founded in 1981 by members of Psychic TV. One of its cofounders, Genesis P-Orridge, believed that communal living was a vital element to magickal development often overlooked.

A key moment in Crowley's esoteric development was his introduction to Eastern thought by his mountaineering guru, Oscar Eckensten, who led the unsuccessful expedition to conquer K2 in 1902, and Allen Bennet, a pioneering monk responsible for introducing the West to Buddhism. Bennet was a leading member of the Golden Dawn, taking Crowley under his wing after introducing himself, looking deeply into Aleister's eyes and announcing, "Little brother, you have been meddling with the Goetia." When Crowley nervously denied dabbling in black magick, he replied, "Then the Goetia has been meddling with you." It was dangerous to work with such forces, they knew, and absolutely pivotal to safeguard oneself through rigorous practices if one did. It didn't matter a fig how much ritual, ceremonial, sexual, black, or white magick you practiced, or how many skeletons you fed blood to (yes, he tried that too). If you didn't have control of your own mind, it was all for nothing in the end.

Eckenstein once had challenged Crowley in Mexico to try to hold a single thought without wandering. He promptly sat and tried to do it, convinced of the strength of his own mind, and was amazed at its utter faithless flaccidity, crying out loud, "By God, you are right!" Buddhist meditation and control of the mind, and then through the mind, eventually the body, was a journey of a thousand steps that simply had to be taken. Far from its familiarity today, yoga and meditation at that time were considered to be part of Esoteric Western Magick. Indeed, Crowley's *Book 4*, in the first part to his magnum opus *Magick*, is a study in Asana positions, mantras, and breath techniques to achieve yogic states of mind.

Crowley took up residence in the highlands of Scotland, at Boleskine House, overlooking Loch Ness. Crowley brought all of his magickal presence there, and he began a narrow focus on conducting a six-month ritual, which followed his reading the instructions in *The Book of the Sacred Magic of Abramelin the Mage*. Stories quickly began to circulate. A man who had been a teetotaler all of his life suddenly went on a bender and killed his entire family with a shotgun. The local butcher, infuriated with Crowley for not paying his bills, was rumored to have been cursed by Crowley. As a consequence, as the story went, he chopped his own hand clean off! Several witnesses saw strange phenomena in or around the property or emanating from it. Crowley himself saw strange forms appearing in the shadows, in corners of his house. Since then, Boleskine House, once owned by Jimmy Page of the band Led Zeppelin, has recently burned to the ground and is scheduled to be rebuilt, using crowdfunding, to make it a place of learning and knowledge, housing a vast occult library. I recommend visiting the eerily beautiful graveyard just below the site if you happen to go by.

Crowley, who loved dressing up and creating characters, lived the part as the Laird of Boleskine much as a method actor would, except with his tongue firmly lodged in his cheek. Much ridicule can be heaped on such acting behavior, but it forces and bends reality. It opens the mind of the person to grow to be more than himself. Chaos magick instruction encourages us to behave in different manners on different given days. In the book *Fight Club*, the members had to pick and start a physical confrontation and then deliberately lose it. The consciousness shift for the victor and the loser is a revelatory one.

A major milestone in Crowley's ambitious achievement list is his writing and publishing of the periodical *The Equinox*. That was important because he attempted the herculean task of synthesizing religion and its practices into a coherent form for mankind to benefit from, something the New Age movement never achieved, and that superhuman effort is outlined in the strapline for it: "The aim of religion, the method of science." For this accomplishment alone, we can look to Crowley as we do the Scottish anthropologist Sir James George Fraser and his magnificent work *The Golden Bough*.

The Equinox can still be bought in its original twelve volumes, supplemented by the rarer *Blue Equinox*. With print-on-demand and the online availability of PDF texts, now the information is more available than ever before. As the late Herman Slater, of the Magickal Childe shop, said, "Everything's in print now." He meant magick is no longer held in the hands of a few elite groups. Glowing phone and laptop screens aside, let us also remember that many of us occultists still love books. The smell of a rare volume in one's hands after months of searching for it, the mystique of finding an annotated front-page dedication to a pupil, or the thrill of finding a note of dedication from a lover from years past feeds our imaginations. Crowley published his magickal works as physical spells, selecting the size, color, and design to expedite the books' messages and enchant the reader further. It's often our passion for the rare and forbidden antiquarian books that led us first to stray into the hidden knowledge we know as occult.

Something happened to Crowley in Egypt in 1904 that would forever alter his path. It was this crucible moment from which he forged Thelema. He received a transmission over three days from an intelligence called Aiwass. That message was dictated to Crowley as *The Book of the Law*. These three chapters formed the basis of Thelema. Initially rejected by Crowley, the manuscript was found hidden away in an attic. Rereading it, he finally embraced its message and accepted his mantle as the book's prophet and High Priest. It's a journey that would consume him for the rest of his life.

Traveling around Egypt with his wife, Rose Kelly, Crowley dressed as Choia Khan, a prince of Persia. In November 1903 they spent a night in the Great Pyramid, in the "King's Chamber," in the center of the structure. Crowley read a ritual to invoke the Ibis-headed god Thoth, intended to fill the chamber with astral light to impress his wife. Exposure to a night in the King's Chamber is said to lead to a profound and personal experience. Indeed, the Sahara Desert sand itself has always had an effect on human consciousness. Its stark beauty and the lack of visual stimulus leads to a tamping down of everyday thought patterns.

On March 16, 1904, Crowley invoked Thoth again, using the IAO formula. He performed the Bornless One ritual, hoping to entertain Rose by showing her the manifestation of sylphs. However, instead of witnessing the sylphs, Rose fell into a trancelike state, hearing intonations without seeing anything. She became intensely excited about the messages she received, which included phrases such as "They are waiting for you" and "It's all about the child." Initially, Crowley was annoyed by these messages and didn't take them seriously.

The following day, Rose spontaneously started uttering more messages without any invocations. By the eighteenth, she believed that Horus was speaking to Crowley through her. This led Crowley to take the messages more seriously, along with other proof of her clairvoyance and indications that the spirit communicating with her could see into his mind. They subsequently visited Cairo's Boulak Museum of Egyptian Antiquities. Though he still had doubts, Crowley smiled wryly as Rose passed cases of statues and images of Horus. He quizzed her further, and without hesitation she led him to an image of Horus on a beautifully painted and colored wooden tablet known as the Stele of Revealing, which amazingly had the exhibit number 666. Later, Rose revealed that it was not Horus, but a messenger named Aiwass who was representing Horus, who spoke through her.

At that time, Crowley himself had grown bored with magick and disheartened with the occult, questioning its purpose, saying, "You see, but what's the point?" and the like. Skeptical of his wife's sudden clairvoyance, he calculated the odds of all these events occurring and was stunned by the implications. As a result, he followed Rose's instructions to eat, dress, and act in specific ways. He became a scribe, not directly for Horus or Ra-Hoor-Khuit, but for the messenger known as Aiwass (or possibly AIWAZZ). Crowley, still skeptical, suspected that the name of the messenger might have been derived from Rose overhearing the Arabic word for "yes," which is "aiwa."

On April 7, despite previous doubts and concerns, at the stroke of noon, and with his trusty Swan fountain pen and quarto sheets of writing paper, Crowley began his role as scribe for this demon, devil, god, guardian angel, or preter-human intelligence that was Aiwass. Crowley was about to usher in "the equinox of the gods." Over the next three days, the 220 verses were dictated to Crowley in three distinct chapters.

During the dictation process, Aleister observed that the voice of Aiwass came from over his left shoulder, from the farthest corner in the room, and it reverberated through his physical heart. The voice was of a deep timber and was musical and expressive, at once tender, fierce, and solemn. It was also uncanny to him that the voice seemed devoid of all traceable accent. The impression was that this was a tall, dark man of fine transparent matter, with the face of a savage Assyrian or Persian king, his eyes veiled to prevent them from destroying whatever they gazed upon.

The dictation was so fast at times that Crowley struggled to keep up, and that is reflected in the messy areas of the handwriting on the original manuscript. It began with Nuit as the speaker, goddess of the sky and the stars (shown on the Stele of Revealing as a blue woman bending over to form a protective arch, reflecting the eternity of the universe), spoken through Aiwass.

The next chapter was dictated from the viewpoint of Hadith, the male aspect of Nuit, although still spoken through Aiwass. Hadith was painted on the stele as a disk with large wings, just below the torso of Nuit. This deity represents the center of the circle, the microcosm within the macrocosm, as a focal point of the universe within us all. The last chapter was dictated on the third and final day. It was a vengeful disrupter in the form of the hawk-headed Horus, which then spoke through Aiwass to his new prophet, Crowley, who had been renamed Prince Ankh-f-n-Khonsu. He bid him to take up the mantle of High Priest and to be an apostle of the new Aeon, "the crowned and conquering child."

This Book of the Law announced the death of Christianity and mainstream religions. As my understanding goes, humans began with the Pagan period, worshiping nature, Isis, and various mother goddesses. Then it was superseded by the worship of man, Osiris, suffering, and death. During this time period, we ignored the physical that makes us human beings, and we focused entirely on the spiritual. The "child of the new aeon," Horus, was a melting pot of both the spiritual and the physical. This law is one of liberty, love, and light. It promised to be the future.

The Book of the Law, or *Liber AL*, as it was later known, was both beautiful and troubling, sublime in its simplicity in some verses, then bafflingly complex in others. The published version always includes a facsimile of the original manuscript in the Beast's own handwriting. Commentary on this "holy book" has been forbidden, and it was considered wise to destroy it after the first reading. I would urgently advise anyone who is considering consuming the book in this way to meditate and prepare themselves as they see fit, to capture a receptive frame of mind. Then I recommend sitting alone in silence to digest the book for themselves. Draw your own conclusions, reader, and make of it what you will.

From the text of this book comes two main principles, "Thelema," Greek for "will," and "Agape," Greek for "a principled and general love for all," as with a divine love.

Do what thou wilt shall be the whole of the law.
Love is the law, love under will.
Every man and woman is a star.

The book advocated locating your unconscious "higher self" and entering into a communication with it, sometimes known as "Conversation with your Holy Guardian Angel." This will lead to discovering your "true will," your real inner motivating source, the very reason for your existence in this world. Then you should act upon it, as the teachings go, and pursue it with a rapturous love, knowing that you have a place in this universe and a responsibility for that given place. We are all divine beings that can unify perfectly with the divinity of the infinite expanse. "A man whose conscious will is at odds with his True Will is wasting his strength." Crowley likens such a man to a nation in a state of civil war. This was, and still is, a system that aims to bring individuals into harmony with themselves and their environment.

Crowley's proclamation for life was perfectly summarized in his manifesto, *Liber OZ*. It included the key verses of *The Book of the Law* (*Liber AL*).

Liber LXXVII
OZ
The law of the strong: this is our law and the joy of the world.
—AL II:21

Do what thou wilt shall be the whole of the Law.
—AL I:40

Thou hast no right but to do thy will. Do that, and no other shall say nay.
—AL I:3

There is no god but man.
1. Man has the right to live by his own law—to live in the way that he wills to do,
2. To work as he will, to play as he will, to rest as he will, to die when and how he will.
3. Man has the right to think what he will, to speak what he will, to write what he will, to draw,
4. paint, carve, etch, mould, build as he will, to dress as he will.
5. Man has the right to love as he will, "take your fill and will of love as ye will, when, where, and with whom ye will."
—AL I:51

Man has the right to kill those who would thwart these rights. "The slaves shall serve."
—AL II:58

Love is the law, love under will.
—AL I:57

In 1909, Crowley and his disciple, Victor Neuburg, were traveling through North Africa. They had formed a close magickal friendship and sexual bond that was to last for years. Victor, a graduate of Cambridge, was a poet and natural seer of the highest ability. He underwent training in the Scottish Highlands at Boleskine House, with Crowley in the role of his guru. Having left civilization at Bou Saada, they had been sleeping under the stars, braving the intense desert sun and possible frostbite from the freezing sands at night. They were armed with a revolver, concealed under Crowley's robes, to deter an Arab ambush. He also carried a wooden Calvary cross of six squares of painted vermillion, set with a large golden topaz. The much-younger Victor Neuburg, or Brother Omnia Vincam ("I shall conquer all"), followed with a rucksack containing writing paper, pens, and several notebooks. His head was shaved, except for two horns of hair painted red, so he resembled a sprite or tamed demon to many.

"A hand smote its lighting" in his heart, and Crowley heard a familiar voice entreating him to go deeper into the desert and "call Me." They both embarked upon a work called *The Vision and the Voice*, utilizing a fascinating system of Elizabethan magick called Enochian. Fortuitously, Victor's notebook contained the "19 calls of the aethers" carefully copied by hand from the manuscripts.

Enochian language and magick was pioneered by Doctor John Dee, who was Queen Elizabeth I's astrologer and advisor. He was also a scientist and mathematician who was prepared to storm the gates of heaven for the ultimate prize, to find the answers of the universe. The church forbade anyone from dabbling with demonic magick. Defiance held dire consequences, but one way to skirt around the rule was the study of "angelic magic," communication with the heavens' hierarchy of angels. Doctor Dee was prepared to create an important system in this way. After careful deliberation, he chose Sir Edward Kelly to be his scryer. He was an imperfect vessel, but he was one who got tangible results anyway. Kelly gazed into a shew stone (a black obsidian mirror) and they made contact with seemingly angelic entities. From 1552 to 1559, through the construction of large grids of letters, the Enochian language was uncovered and meticulously recorded. Like Michelangelo chipping away at a block of stone, releasing the carving of an angel trapped in its core, this language had its own syntax and grammar and was entirely unique, having come into existence on Earth only as it was divined from "angels." The study of this system can expand one's mind before even fully engaging with it, many have felt.

> The thirty aethyrs, whose dominion extendeth in ever-widening circles beyond the watchtowers of the universe.
>
> 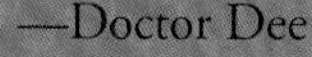
>
> —Doctor Dee

The Thirty Keys (or calls) symbolize the fourth-dimensional universe in two dimensions as a square surrounded by concentric circles, one inside the other, radiating outward. It forms a Great Work for the aspiring magician. Through the rigorous scrying work, often begrudgingly performed by Kelly (griping over money or being tired), they delved deeper and deeper. Kelly worried about the "angels" being, in fact, demons in disguise. These ideas were brushed aside by Dee in his vaulting ambition. However, at one point they asked the question directly, and they received the disturbing reply that there's "no difference."

The pair embarked on many adventures, trusting the "angelic" conversations to guide their lives, gaining audiences with Rudolf II at his palace in Prague, and with King Stephen Bathory of Poland. Their story ended rather tragically, though. Dee's hopes of an ultimate key of knowledge that united and unlocked the universe was ended by the final "angelic" message, which was to share all of their possessions (including their wives). Reluctantly, Kelly and Dee carried out the instructions, and at one point Dee returned to England to find his library, the largest private collection in Britain, ransacked. He found his reputation in tatters, and his wife pregnant, possibly with Kelly's child. Sir Edward Kelly stayed behind in the employ of Rudolf (in Prague). He became trapped there by his own scheme: He was caught in a far-wider political design than he bargained for, to make gold from lead, a false work of alchemists.

The shew stone and the beautiful wax tablets used by Kelly and Dee can still be seen on display in the British Museum, in London. Don't forget to peek in the Atlantis Bookshop while there if you should happen to visit the museum, since it's just around the corner.

Crowley's work on the Enochian system took the Golden Dawn's initial teachings and elucidated them much further than they could have imagined, by going back to the raw source material of Doctor John Dee, found in the British Library, and using his practical exploration of the "thirty aethyrs" extensively. These have given us the cohesive modern magickal system that stands today. A wax cylinder recording of Crowley reading the calls, as well as him singing "Vive la France," makes for fascinating listening.

In the desert, Crowley and Neuburg worked together to complete the system of Enochian calls. Aleister was using the topaz as a gazing stone, with Victor as the scribe, at times furiously writing to keep up with his master's dictation. The text described the visions he was experiencing. On one call, they had their path blocked, and they pushed through with an act of sex magick. That left a profound impression on Crowley as to its potential uses.

The tenth aethyr, called Zax, was guarded by what Kelly said was a "mighty Devil called Chronozon." Amid the dunes, they marked out a circle inscribed with the holy names of God to fortify it. That was for Victor's protection. Away from the circle was traced a triangle with the name of Chronozon in its center, and along the sides were more names of God to prevent the demon from breaking out. Three doves were sacrificed, their blood in each of the corners of the triangle providing a source of power for the entity to manifest after the evocation. Crowley took the unprecedented step of kneeling in the thunderbolt hatha yoga position inside the triangle, where the demon was to appear! He called forth Chronozon, to be evoked within himself as well as on the physical plane.

Crowley became possessed by Chronozon, and they opened the "gates of hell" by using the words uttered by Adam, "Zasas Zasas Nasatanada Zasas." Chronozon tempted Victor to leave the protection of his circle, appearing as a beautiful and seductive woman that Victor had once known, mimicking her voice perfectly. When that failed, the demon appealed to Victor's mercy, crying out in the anguished voice of Crowley, begging for water to quench his thirst. Finally, at the ritual's climax, Chronozon deliberately distracted the scribe (Victor) by increasing its insane and furious dictation. As he desperately tried to keep up with the deranged babble, his frenetic handwriting disintegrated and left the page altogether. The demonized Crowley seized that moment to escape the confinement of the triangle, and it traversed the sand between them by leaping straight into the protective circle and attacking Victor with its teeth, only to be warded off with his dagger. After their adventures in exploring the Enochian aethyrs, Crowley invariably fell out with Victor, as he was wont to do, and he abandoned him to die in the desert. On his return to civilization, when asked what became of Victor, he silently pointed to his ex-companion's empty camel saddle.

Surviving that episode, Victor Neuburg formed the independent Vine Press, edited "The Poet's Corner," and published some truly beautiful poetry, including "The Triumph of Pan," and was responsible for being the literary godfather to Dylan Thomas, who said, "Vicky encouraged me as no one else has done. . . . He possessed many kinds of genius, and not the least was his genius for drawing to himself, by his wisdom, graveness, great humor, and innocence—a feeling of trust and love that won't ever be forgotten." Incidentally, Timothy Leary, famed as "the godfather of LSD," while traveling in North Africa, found that he was following in Crowley's exact footsteps through the deserts, as if in a past life, and he identified with synchronistic similarities in his own life's trajectory and Crowley's.

A tap on Crowley's door one night in 1912 opened another gateway in his life. The mysterious stranger who appeared, sporting a handlebar moustache and pince-nez glasses, turned out to be a high-ranking German Freemason, a member of the German Secret Service, and head of a magickal order called the Ordo Templi Orientis, the Temple of the East, or

O.T.O., as it has often been commonly called. The gentleman's name was Theodor Reuss, and he had a "bone to pick" with Crowley. After the fourteenth Enochian aethyr call, which had needed a sexual act to allow further progress, Crowley had been formulating and speculating on the idea that sex and all its vital energy, coupled with the magician's will, through directed thought or visualization, may hold the central key to the Great Work.

Theodor Reuss accused Crowley of revealing his order's innermost secret; namely, the "IX Secret." Crowley was actually a recent member of the O.T.O., from one year earlier. He had been a collector of memberships to secret societies, in much the manner of a rare book collector. Since he hadn't attained the ninth grade, to access the IX secret, how could he possibly have revealed it? Reuss took down Crowley's recently published volume *The Book of Lies* from the shelf and opened it at the page that began "Let the adept be armed with his Magickal Rood and provided with his Mystic Rose." Crowley may have meant "rood" to be old English for rod, used when referring to a crucifix, but, thinking on his feet, he realized that the secret ninth degree of the O.T.O. was sexual in nature. The two men talked long into the night, pooling secrets involving a branch of Hindu practice known as tantra, the use of talismans consecrated with sexual secretions and charged with prana energy. Crowley was quickly offered the position as head of the British branch of the O.T.O. He traveled to Berlin to be initiated, and he took the magickal name of Baphomet, the title of the secret idol the "Knights Templar" were accused of worshiping (which was really a creation of the church to defame the prophet Muhammad and discourage Islamic conversions, originally). He immediately set about rewriting the order's rituals to embrace the tenets of *The Book of the Law*, naturally.

In tantric legends, the saints were often initiated by women, the power holders, experienced temple dancers, or prostitutes. Crowley, with his strong masochistic streak, loved experienced women, and he saw his Scarlet Women as literally embodying the Great Goddess. Crowley's discovery of sex magick brought together two pillars of his life, to be a powerful and famous magician like no other, and to be a notorious sexual athlete.

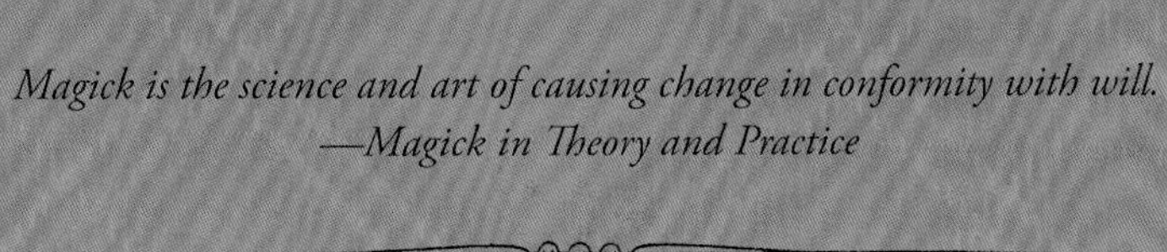

Magick is the science and art of causing change in conformity with will.
—Magick in Theory and Practice

Crowley's definition of what magick actually is has never been surpassed. He added the "K" to separate stage magic from occult magick. The letter *K* in Hebrew means to "bend" or "tame," and for Crowley it also has a sexual connotation. Find two meanings in his work and you've often missed another three. The more modern interpretation adds "in consciousness" after "causing change." This somewhat negates the idea that magick can cause change in the physical world. If our minds are miniature maps of the universe, and if they are connected to the universe, couldn't a large enough shift in the microcosm (our brain) within the macrocosm (the entire universe) cause a perceptible synchronistic change in physical matter? Theoretically, it's a sound scientific principle, and it certainly finds some support in the newer field of quantum physics today, such as in the changes found in the behavior of photons when observed, versus when not observed.

Conventional ceremonial magick takes lengthy preparation with the disciplined use of set rituals, utilizing rare or expensive materials. Chaos magickians, on the other hand, have seen no importance in how one achieves an altered state, and have been comfortable with using any tools that fire the imagination, even fictional books such as the *Necronomicon*. It's the state of mind one is able to achieve, by any means necessary, that has mattered for them.

Sex magick democratizes magick by placing in our hands, literally in our bodies, all the power we need. By specific acts of sex, one can bring about change in the physical world. Our bodies become the temple. Sexual secretions become the sacrament. Our sexual organs are seen as living symbols of what the archetypal symbols stand for, like the wand and the cup. The act of sex becomes a communion with God, with our higher self, or our holy guardian angel, or the deep unconscious that drives us all. In sex magick, the "spell" is to hold an image in your mind of what you are requesting, be it a mental picture or a personal sigil prepared earlier. Keeping the image in your mind throughout the moment of orgasm and then releasing it into the universe, you then forget about the whole thing. Think nothing of it again, having complete faith that the result has been achieved. Working "without the lust of result" is the way, for who can recall a specific orgasm? Just leave it all in the lap of the gods and move on, so your mind cannot begin to sow doubt. Doubt is the antithesis of success.

Sex magick, often called the left-hand path, folds space rather like passing through a black hole / wormhole to emerge from another hole, having instantly traversed across unimaginable distances in space and time. The orgasm, or "the little death" as the French call it, is a powerful miniature DMT-like experience. As the orgasm blows our minds, it makes a little dent or hole in the fabric of the universe itself. For Crowley, it was a recovering and unstopping of the Dionysian fountain long denied by Christendom.

At the height of his power and belief in the Law of Thelema, in 1920, Crowley and his small group of followers founded the Abbey of Thelema in a farmhouse in Cefalù, Sicily. He chose Cefalù after consulting the I Ching, a method of Chinese divination using eight trigrams. Any doubts his disciples might have had were dispersed on arrival—it was idyllically perfect to establish a spiritual commune and practice the religion of Thelema as free men and women. At this point, we should consider what they were trying to achieve within the context of the period, which was already being called the "age of impotence." Much of Crowley's doctrine advocated personal freedom, complete liberation. In 1920, this attitude was far ahead of its time, preempting the movement of the 1960s by some forty years, with free love, drugs, music, and art exploding on the scene. This also led to him being revered as a 1960s icon, eternally represented on the Beatles' *Sergeant Pepper* album cover.

Life at the Abbey began with group worship of the sun every morning. Days were spent in creative pursuit, through painting, writing, climbing the Rocca that overlooks Cefalù, swimming in the sea, meditation, and performing magickal tasks laid down by Crowley in order for each person to discover their true will. Between these times, household chores were carried out and meals were taken in silence after saying "Will," a Thelemic form of grace. This was to keep the diners focused on finding or pursuing their true will. Magickal diaries were kept meticulously. These were highly personal accounts of thoughts, impressions, dreams, and any magickal practices to further individual development, such as cutting oneself with a razor every time one used the word "I." Only Crowley was allowed access to read these records at any time, monitoring progress and giving advice in his role as Holy Guru.

Contrary to popular belief, the locals were not hostile to the magician and his followers, sometimes climbing the hill to take them bread and olives. The local barber did a good trade in shaving the male Thelemites' heads, leaving the signature little phallic lock of hair in the front. The Abbey had no running water, but it wasn't the unsanitary hovel described by some. However, life could be, at times, far from halcyon. Jealous fights broke out among the women. Accusations of evil magick abounded after Poupée (Anne Leah), Crowley's much-loved daughter, died. Disciples grew tired of Aleister's "holier than thou" attitude. Drugs, including heroin and cocaine, were so freely available, as were tobacco and alcohol, that even children were allowed to try them. This led to inevitable addictions and their accompanying problems. A spying Scottish journalist took advantage of their faultier nature and paved the way for their downfall by writing malicious and salacious stories for the hungry British press.

After the sad death of disciple Raoul Loveday, his partner, Betty May, revealed an exposé account of her stay at the Abbey to the papers. Things quickly unraveled, culminating in the Thelemites' expulsion from Sicily and the subsequent loss of the Abbey. In the twilight of his life, Crowley wrote that his stay at the Abbey of Thelema had been one of the happiest times of his life. An idealized account of the *Collegium ad Spiritum Sanctum*, as Crowley called it, can be read in the outrageously titled novel *The Diary of a Drug Fiend*. Crowley dictated it in one draft over the course of a number of days. It's a rather sobering tale of two young lovers trapped in a hellish purgatory of addiction, who eventually seek recovery from their self-destructive impulses at the Abbey of Thelema. Under the instruction of Basil King Lamus, they discover their true will and are liberated from their drug enslavement.

In 1996, I rediscovered the Abbey and spent time removing the whitewash from the walls to photograph the paintings underneath. No one had really been inside since filmmaker Kenneth Anger, in the 1950s. His incredible work preserved paintings on window shutters and doors, and those lying on the floor and flung outside the Abbey. My own work documented the paintings in the so-called "chamber of nightmares," photographed in color for the first time. The room depicted a goat copulating with a scarlet-haired woman. It showed the feet of Aiwass dancing on the earth, the "blind and degenerate" god, sporting a huge erection with a single eye set in a livid yellow head. The phrase "Stab your demonic smile to my brain, soak me in cognac, cunt, and cocaine" ran down the length of one wall. The murals were designed to shock the viewers, and to help shed their shame around sex. The choice of bright colors and strange perspectives, psychedelic and striking, stemmed partly from Crowley sniffing ether between brushstrokes. I also gathered firsthand stories of what happened at the Abbey, such as someone witnessing Crowley free-climbing the Rocca, with nothing but a bag of chalk dust for grip, stripped to the waist, with blood running from his fingers and dripping from his elbows before reaching the summit. I heard tales of him whipping his followers, tied to two pillar stones at the front of the house, to keep a sense of discipline. I also learned that the group's expulsion by Mussolini was, in fact, orchestrated by the local archbishop, who detested Crowley and what he stood for, living as a "free man." My return from Cefalù culminated in a Channel 4 documentary series called *The Masters of Darkness*.

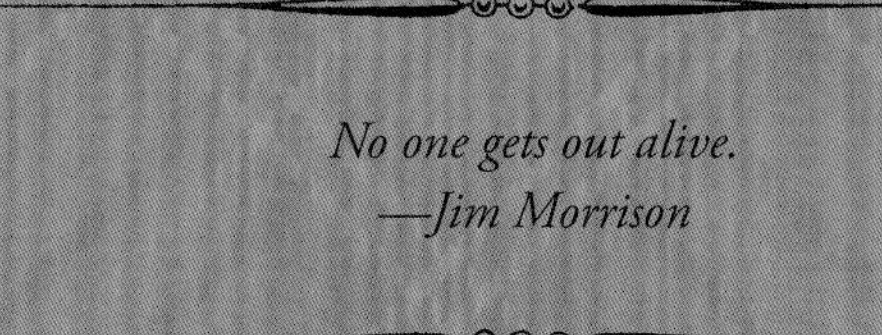

No one gets out alive.
—Jim Morrison

The dark legacy of the 1960s and the excesses of rock and roll was one of mental illness, drug addiction, and death. Many of Crowley's followers who got out found sobriety and a new god of their understanding. They were the lucky ones, who tragically had to watch as their friends and colleagues in the music industry died of drug overdoses or alcoholism on a daily basis. With the age of the internet, illegal drugs are more freely available than ever before. Drugs to induce alternate states of mind can be useful if applied to a specific purpose. Microdosing LSD is a common end of the spectrum; the Third Reich used methamphetamine to fuel its "blitzkrieg," or lightning warfare.

Crowley knew that no two drugs produced the same results. His book *777*, based on the Golden Dawn teachings, included the addition of different chemical substances as part of the table of correspondences attached to the Tree of Life. He even added mace before it was recognized as a psychoactive substance, to aid magickal practice. However, be warned: Experimentation can lead to addiction very quickly. The mercurial heights of altered consciousness are only temporary. Addiction is not a war to be won by the strength of your conscious will. It's an insidious war with your core self. If a drug "clicks" with you, seeming to reveal a truth within you, it may also be feeding a growing need within you. A drug cannot be conquered intellectually, or by repeatedly taking it.

Crowley was addicted to heroin, and he tried many times to free himself. Read Steve Wilson's edition of *Liber TzBa* for further insight on that. Crowley was also deeply perturbed by his cravings for cocaine. In his *Magickal Diaries*, not written for publication or general consumption, he actually questions the validity of *The Book of the Law*. In particular, lines from verse 22: "Worship me, take wine and strange drugs, whereof I will tell my prophet, and be drunk thereof! They shall not harm ye at all. It is a lie." He couldn't conceivably admit that he was an addict, because it's not possible if you have found your True Will, let alone if you were the chosen prophet of liberty, where "the word of sin is restriction." If you drank fine cognac, fucked, and sniffed the purest cocaine, and it was part of your true will, it could do you harm. Yet, at the Abbey of Thelema, his five-year-old son became addicted to smoking cigarettes. Devotees arrived at the Abbey healthy but left as addicts, not the other way around. Later in his life, when the 1920 Dangerous Drugs Act kicked in and heroin couldn't be bought over the counter, a relative told me that his landlady kept finding empty gin bottles all over his residence. In the letters to Freida Harris, his paranoia over money and copyright regarding their work on the Tarot, she felt, was exacerbated by his bouts of drinking. Crowley lived the heroin life, the opium life, and the cocaine life, as he called it, but you don't need to risk becoming addicted to prove you're not an addict in order to confirm your true will.

Crowley has become mythic through his lifestyle and teachings, and his iconic face in photographs and paintings have nearly made him a Jungian archetype. His image can remind us of what can be achieved in a single lifetime. He represents something missing in religion, something very human that we need. A renegade Buddha, an antihero, a gangster prophet riding a Cadillac drawn by swans . . . with rouged cheeks and gold earrings, he was the son of Lucifer, the fallen angel, made flesh on Earth. He was Sorath, the spirit of the sun. Awaiss, Set, Shaitan, or Satan was Crowley's guardian angel with a message for all mankind. He thought this intelligence was an ipsissimus, a pure spirit of highest self, at one with the universe. This was a level of existence Crowley himself claimed to have reached.

Alexander Cabot, the author of this book, is a man at the very coal face of modern magick today. He was contacted by, and conversed with, the entity called Crowley through his dreams. No one has claimed to be a reincarnation of the Beast as far as we know, so perhaps we can raise aloft our copy of the "Stele of Revealing" and gaze at the wreathed portrait of the Great Beast, as Jimmy Page did in Kenneth Anger's film *Lucifer Rising*. Maybe it's our time to commune with him as a deity in his own right.

What is Crowley's legacy, aside from sex, drugs, and theatrics (such as filing his teeth into points to give women the "serpent's kiss," defecating on floors or stairs of people he felt had slighted him, or the insanely hot curries he made, so incandescent that people fainted at dinner parties)? Crowley's influence has revived and shaped the entire Western magickal tradition as we know it today. In the realm of Wicca, Gerald Gardner's *Book of Shadows* remains the standard manual for the modern craft, put together with himself and Crowley. It's a beautiful blend of Thelema and Dianic worship. Take the section known as "The Charge," for example: "Listen to the words of the Great

Mother, who of old was called among men Artemis, Astarte, Diana, Melusine, Ceridwen, Arianrod, Baich, and by many other names. . . . As a sign that ye shall be really free, ye shall be naked in your rites, and ye shall dance, sing, make love—all in praise of me. For Mine is the ecstacy of the spirit and Mine is the joy on earth, for My law is Love under Will."

Modern Satanism skirted around Crowley, largely because of his complexity, and went on to dabble in Nazi occultism but emerged to embrace the practice of magick with its own powerfully charged Satanic current. The O.T.O. thrives today, as do many other Thelemic-based organizations. The Tarot deck, from its humble woodcut origins, now has the spectacular Thoth deck, designed by Crowley toward the end of his life, painted in incredible detail and colors by Freda Harris. It's an essential pack, used by Tarot readers who often are unaware of its influences.

His image and ideas appear in many contemporary novels, comics, and films, including the recent screen adaptation of *Good Omens* by Terry Pratchet and Neil Gamen, featuring a devil called Crowley working with an angel called Aziraphale. Nick Hedges produced Shakespeare's *The Tempest* for the London stage and set it in Cefalù, with Crowley as Prospero. Kenneth Anger's long-awaited film of Crowley's *Gnostic Mass* is set to be another seminal piece of cinema soon. All around the globe, we occultists owe a debt of gratitude to the Mega Therion.

Crowley, the man, died on December 1, 1947. Different accounts of that moment are as follows: that he died crying, tears rolling down his cheeks, uttering the last words "I am perplexed" or "I am confused," or that while on his death bed, Crowley cursed the doctor, who refused him more morphine, and that the doctor died the next day. A much-simpler version is that his landlady at Netherwood heard a heavy thump on the ceiling above her and then went upstairs to find the Beast collapsed dead on the floor.

I was lucky enough to have worked on an interview with the last "scarlet woman" alive, Deidre MacAlpine. Her account, as she was actually there, is that he slipped into a coma after spending time with her and their son, talking and laughing, with his last known words being "Oh, sometimes I hate myself." The moment he passed from life into death, on that still winter's day, the room's curtains suddenly blew up through the open window and remained pinned to the ceiling for a moment. She felt sure it was the gods who had come to take him home. Freed from the prison of life, and like Jesus's ascension into heaven, he truly became the ipsissimus, the man who escaped Samsara to become the myth that is Aleister Crowley today.

He was cremated in Brighton on Friday, December 5, and a handful of friends and admirers attended the funeral. It caused a mild outrage with the local authorities, due to the hymn to Pan being recited, a powerful invocation to the god of nature, along with excerpts from *The Book of the Law*. This gnostic requiem was read by his friend Louis Wilkinson, a man whose voice became the world's first live television broadcast from Alexander Palace, London. Crowley had wanted to be buried on top of the Rocca in Cefalù, at the foot of a cliff behind Boleskine House, or interred in Westminster Abbey, or even to be mummified. His ashes have actually been lost or possibly stolen, and so perhaps he got, at least, an earlier wish: "Bury me in a nameless grave."

> My life has been a delirious dance to maddening music, with incarnate passion for my partner. I have attained all my ambitions, proved myself at every point, dared every danger, enjoyed the ecstasy that life has to offer. From this look upon life with enlightened eyes, I sought and found, and then I set out to seek those who seek, that they might also find.
>
> —Aleister Crowley

Was he a false messiah, as his close friend Gerald Yorke called him? He was certainly a deeply flawed one, and from his own diaries, he knew this to be true himself, but if anyone is in doubt as to his sincerity, I'd like to end this article with a paragraph of his writing that reflects his life's work. It rings as true now, in the online world we inhabit, as it was the moment he put pen to paper:

> No one can be indifferent to the mysteries of life and death. Those who still respect honest thought and who have not yet succumbed to the radio, the cinema, and the headline, are bound to read what is certain to help mankind, as individuals and as a race, to substitute sanity and happiness for the crazy misery which is, at present, the lot for the vast majority of us.

Love is the law, love under will.
—Aron Paramor

The world breaks everyone, and afterward, many are strong at the broken places.
—Ernest Hemingway

CHAPTER 4
PAPA ACHE

The first time I experienced an African religion was when I was thirteen. At that time, I was one of the few Cubans of European descent who participated in this faith. The specific African diaspora religious tradition was Palo Monte (a term no longer used). The word "Monte" refers to the woods.

RAUL

I had a dear Afro-Cuban friend named Raul who was exiled from Spain to the United States. He started his first year with me in the fifth grade. He stood out to me because he wore all white, as a promise to the spirits (Saints of Santeria) made to preserve his health. At that time, there was racial prejudice in the Cuban culture. My mother and grandmother mentioned their racially biased standpoint to me, but I was always color blind. I saw people of all colors to potentially be loving, wonderful people. (As a sidenote: I always knew that the key to the evolution of the human species is to mix with as much variety as possible—the opposite of the birth defects experienced when close relatives have children.)

Raul and I immediately clicked. Raul would, in time, become one of my closest and dearest friends. Not too long after we became friends, I was invited to go play at his house. While there, I met his entire family: his sisters, his brothers, his mother, and his father.

RENÉ

I learned early on that Raul's father, René Villarreal, was a jeweler who worked in the diamond district in Manhattan. One day, while I was with Raul at his house, someone informed me that René practiced Palo Mayombe (originally a pretty dark art, a type of necromancy, but later "Christianized" to provide a much less intimidating stigma), and he had to complete a mission that he had promised to do for Spirit. If he failed to keep his promise, he would lose his eyesight. Because of my magickal heritage, I found that mission to be intriguing. He had been tasked to fashion "la prenda de fundamento," a type of cauldron that holds the *kiyumba*, which is usually bone fragments or the skeletal remains used to entrap or enslave the spirit of the individual the bones belonged to, which again had become more ethical over time, specifically involving ancestors or other "willing" spirits.

Me with Raul Villarreal, Union City, New Jersey, Christmas 1975

René managed to transport an amulet, called a *macuto*—a representation of *la ngangas*, containing the bone fragment of his godfather Papa Ache (a name I would later call René, since he became my godfather in turn). Back in Cuba, René was a shoe cobbler for a while. In those days, people would often wear platform shoes. He was able to hollow out the heel of one of those shoes as a concealed compartment to store the amulet. He managed to do this correctly, flawlessly. This allowed him to smuggle the amulet out of Cuba without it being detected by the Cuban militia. The amulet journeyed from Cuba to Madrid, Spain, and then to the United States. He knew that one day he would have to use that amulet to create "la prenda de fundamento."

RENÉ'S INTRODUCTION TO PALO

Fascinated to learn more about Palo Mayombe, I listened with rapt attention as René relayed the following story to me. He told me about the time in Cuba, around the 1940s, when he had been initiated into his spiritual path. To understand this, it was important to note that he was one of two identical twins. One day, in his youth, while he was playing, two high priests of Santeria (Lucumi) targeted him for a ritual, because he was an identical twin, one they believed was filled with immense magickal power. The priests wished to use René to save a fellow Santero who was spiritually afflicted. René did not know at that time that the price for consenting to do this ritual would be so great. When the priests told him that they needed him to do this work and that they would pay him to do so, he agreed to do it.

Later that day, René went home with the few coins he had been given by the priests. It was not long before he started to become reclusive, depressed, and physically ill. His mother, having knowledge of Santeria, decided to take René to the woods to meet with a Chief High Priest (Padre en Nganga) named Papa Ache. Papa Ache lived in a "barracón" (bunk house), a structure shaped like an equilateral cross to symbolize the four quarters, with four entrances. The center of the bunkhouse served as Papa Ache's living area and place of spiritual workings. There was a little hole in the bottom of the door at the north side of the bunkhouse. René's mother knocked on that door, and a snake came out of the hole. It wrapped itself around the feet of all invited guests, and then it would uncoil itself and go back in (the trick was for one not to be fearful when this happened). This snake act served as a type of cleansing that had to take place prior to anyone entering the bunkhouse. Several moments after the snake disappeared back through the hole in the door, the door would open slightly, and Papa Ache allowed René and his mom to enter the bunkhouse and to proceed into the center court of the barracón. Papa Ache informed René's mother, with his divination, what was wrong with her child and how that came to be.

There was a ritual that needed to be done to save René's life. His mother agreed to go through with the ritual, as Papa Ache had suggested. When the ritual was completed, René was able to regurgitate this mass of hair, which was full of darkness, from his stomach. It was quite a phenomenon! He then started to feel better. René did not yet know that in the future, he would receive the legacy of his godfather (Papa Ache) and learn the traditional magickal practice of Palo Mayombe.

MORE ON PALO MAYOMBE

Palo Mayombe is a religion from the African diaspora (originating in the Congo) that deals with necromancy practices. Palo was a highly controversial and dangerous practice in its beginning, but it later became more orthodox and served the good of all. It was proven to be thus because René's life was saved by it. To comprehend why, one must know that the spirits of Palo Mayombe are those dealing with nature (they are similar to the spirits invoked in Santeria). These spirits work at lower vibrational frequencies, but they are natural and can be quite helpful.

By the time René was fully schooled and initiated, he was a full-fledged adult. It was then that he worked at Ernest Hemingway's estate. Hemingway was a famous American author of the twentieth century, and he lived at his estate in San Francisco de Paula, Cuba, known as Finca Vigia (the Lookout House) from 1939 to 1960. René became Hemingway's butler, friend, and aide (*su hijo Cubano*). Although it is commonly taught at university that Hemingway was an atheist and an adamant existentialist, he was actually an initiated practitioner of Palo Mayombe. There were secret gatherings of Palo practitioners at Hemingway's estate.

René was married to a wonderful Afro-Cuban woman. He used to bring her to the estate. His time spent with Hemingway would be later penned down by René and Raul Villarreal in a book titled *Hemingway's Cuban Son: Reflections on the Writer by His Longtime Majordomo* (Kent State University Press, 2011).

Once René was able to retrieve the aforementioned bone fragment, he left the estate and Cuba behind, because he did not want his family to be brought up under the Communist doctrine of Castro.

I was René's first and youngest godchild of his practice in the United States. When I was thirteen years old, he initiated me into Palo Mayombe. He did a "registro," a spiritual registry for me. There were three energies that came to claim me at the registry (the number three is mercurial and often appears in various places within African-style readings), but only one came to wear her crown for me. The first one was Mama Centella (Remolino Quatro Viento, the equivalent of Oya, which translates to "the swirling four winds"). The second one was Mama Chola, the equivalent of Ochun. The third one was Mama Kalunga, equivalent to Yemaya, Orisha of the oceanic depths according to some lore, and of the graveyard in some older tales. Mama Kalunga was the one who wore her crown for me, claiming me as her child.

René crafted two amulets for me: *el collar de bandera*, "the necklace of the gods," and a *garabato*. The garabato is a scepter that he carved for me from his talented hands. The scepter bore the colors and the face of the spirit Nkuyo Malongo, who is equivalent to Elegua in Santeria.

On occasion, he would have rituals in the room where *la prenda de fundamento* was kept. This cauldron that housed the spirit was placed on a plank where he had soil from many areas, and that plank had wheels. (In order for it to be authentic, it had to be on earth.) Several sacrifices were made, and then the animals were consumed. The element of blood is very powerful in magick. People tend to have the misconception that blood magick is evil, but the animals are consumed, and the blood is considered sacred, not much different from the animal sacrifices of early Israelites. This is a more intimate and careful process than the wanton slaughter of animals for food industries today, and the meat is much safer to consume, as is the case with "kosher" or "halal" meats. The blood is used as an energy source. Other items from the animals are used as well. *Las visoras* (the animal organs) are used for spiritual workings. For an example, the skins of goats are used for creating drums.

Circa late 1970s, the Villarreal family opened up a local botánica (Hispanic occult shop). In it, they sold medicinal herbs and religious goods (this kind of shop is actually quite common in Hispanic or Latino communities). The store was called Papa Ache. It was a corner store that was angled in such a way that it faced the four corners of the street. René's wife was regularly seen behind the counter, selling goods. The whole family would take turns tending the store. I would even help out in the store because I was there so often. I truly loved that store and the family!

There were many times when we congregated at Papa Ache to have spiritual experiences. This would happen in the store's "cuarto de la prenda," the consultation room (where René kept la prenda de fundamento). It was in that room that René would work divination via his Mpaka en Nganga. That was a horn full of secrets, made from the horn of a bull, antelope, or goat, filled with herbs, minerals, and dirt from various locations. The Mpaka en Nganga was used for divination or for entrapping or compelling a spirit. One interesting point is that it was forbidden for a woman to enter that room while menstruating, since her powerful feminine energies could overpower the masculine energetic environment. He often cleansed the entire store, including the consultation room, with cigar smoke or a live rooster.

I recall sessions in the cuarto de la prenda, where Spirit would speak to me via René. He would always comfort me, saying I was a good student. At the age of thirteen, Spirit gave me a profound message that proved to be true. Spirit said that I would experience a sudden change in my life, and Spirit also predicted that later in life, I would be working in an operating room! Today, my profession is in surgical services.

René, whom I called Papa Ache out of respect, taught me certain ways of Spirit. One such way was how to call in the native tongue of the Congo. I wanted him to make me a traditional representation of Nkuyo Malongo. So, I brought him a store-bought concrete vessel meant for Elegua to inhabit. He asked me if my mother would permit me to have one. Even though I knew she had not, and would not have, given me permission to own one, I told Papa Ache that she had given me permission. Knowing I was lying, Spirit shook his head. Papa Ache was furious with me! This was the first time he was mad with me that I can recall.

One day, I remember sitting down and hearing the words of Papa Ache. He delighted my young heart with the stories of a secret order called the Arará. Arará is an African diaspora religion native to Cuba, originating in the colonial era and confined to a secret society of men. Much like the loa are worshiped in Vodou, the luases are honored in the Arará faith. In addition to Vodou, there is also a strong Santeria presence in Arará. Arará refers to a certain land area in Africa. A clandestine group of Ngangas/Paleros (Congo-tradition high priests), the Arará was composed of men who worked their magick via necromancy in a secret location to abolish slavery. They wanted freedom, and their spiritual workings undoubtedly helped with their antislavery goals.

My father, unfamiliar with the Villarreal family and their ways, was concerned for my well-being. My parents were getting a divorce, and I had been spending more time with the Villarreals than with my own biological family. One day, my father came hoping to see me at the store, but I was not there at that time. My Papa Ache greeted my father. They began talking. Father explained his concerns. To this, Papa Ache replied, saying, "Alexander is well protected. No harm will come to him. His name is within the cauldron. He is one of mine, my own." My father breathed a sigh of relief. He was happy to know that I was okay.

So it was that my father became okay with my association with the Villarreal family. My mother, however, did not. She was not happy about it due to her racial bias. I learned that life has a tendency to shift and change. So, against my wishes, I was forced to depart from them and from my mother. As an adolescent, I moved to Miami for two years. My heart was broken because I had a great love for the Villarreals. Thankfully, via modern technology, I was eventually able to reconnect with Raul.

In 2003, I rekindled my relationship with Raul through Classmates.com. Upon reuniting with him, I found out that the loft space that served as his living quarters with his wife, a Cuban American woman, and

Raul, my mother, and I

his artist's studio was the same location as the former great lodge of Freemasonry that my father, mother, and I had attended in my youth. What a small world! As it turned out, he later had to sell it to the city because of eminent domain.

We were excited to reconnect! He invited me over to his home, ironically located only a few blocks from where I lived. At one point during the visit, Raul exclaimed, "Wow! I have had an epiphany. Now I know who this sketch belongs to." Puzzled, I said, "What sketch?" Raul then left to retrieve the drawing he had done. When I saw it, I gasped! The picture featured the same entity who had manifested herself to me years before as one of my guides. This guide was a novice, a postulant who was to become a nun, who had died at an early age. In Raul's sketch, she was holding a white dove. When my guide first manifested herself to me, she had transformed herself into a white dove. Raul told me that he created that sketch years before he handed it to me. At the time, he knew he had to give it to someone, but he was unaware of who until I showed up that day for a visit. I was touched by Goddess that she would use my beloved friend to do this for me! Raul then took the sketch and dedicated it to me with the following words: "*Para mi hermano, la vida, la sangre, mi hermano*. Raul." ["*For my brother, the life, the blood, my brother.* Raul."]

Raul's sketch of my novice spirit guide

The world is not prepared yet to understand the philosophy of Occult Sciences—let them assure themselves first of all that there are beings in an invisible world, whether spirits of the dead or elementals; and that there are hidden powers in man, which are capable of making a God of him on earth.

—H. P. Blavatsky

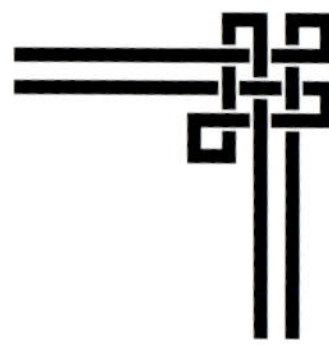

CHAPTER 5
SPIRITUALISM

In the nineteenth century, the United States experienced significant spiritual movements. Tent revivalism really took off in the early 1800s, especially due to the 1700s efforts of early Methodists such as John Wesley and George Whitefield. This encouraged Christians to focus on their salvation and spiritual lives separate from the traditional Catholic Church and Anglican Church. Many Protestant denominations formed around that time, during the period known as the Second Great Awakening. By the mid-1800s, upstate New York would become the birthplace of movements such as Mormonism (1820s) and Spiritualism (1840s).

The Fox sisters (Kate, Leah, and Maggie) are considered to be the ones who began Spiritualism in their home in upstate New York. They claimed that when they would ask spirits of the dead to make their presence known, the spirits would tap on the walls and the ceilings. The sisters, through their conversations with spirits, developed a type of Morse code language for communicating with the dead. For instance, when asked a "yes or no" question, the spirit would be asked to tap once for "yes" and twice for "no."

Andrew Jackson Davis, a renowned seer and academic, taught about the frequencies that spirits communicate to other bodies during life and with each other in higher dimensions. Davis is considered to be a kind of "John the Baptist of Spiritualism," the one who helped lead the way to Spiritualism. He was fascinated by the Fox sisters and their energetic communication with the spirits from beyond the grave. So, he invited them to his home to demonstrate their mediumship abilities.

The Fox sisters began to exercise their mediumship abilities on tour for the masses. Many Christians (engaged in / familiar with the aforementioned Second Great Awakening) became open to practicing Spiritualism, because it helped them feel a sense of authority on their own spirits and their destination after death. Séances began popping up in homes across the country. They did not see a problem with practicing Christianity along with Spiritualism.

Two of these Christian Spiritualists were the famous Sir Arthur Conan Doyle, author for *The Strand* of the famous Sherlock Holmes stories, and his second wife, Jean Doyle. Sir Doyle became an avid supporter of the Spiritualist movement after he had studied Spiritualism for nearly three decades. Jean developed the skill of automatic writing, the act by which a medium is able to transcribe the words of the deceased, allowing the spirit to move their hand and do the writing for them. The Doyles sought lots of support to prove that Spiritualism was real, despite the claims by many that it was all a fraud. To be sure, there were some charlatans about, tipping tables and getting accomplices to knock on walls, which raised skeptical suspicions further.

One of the people who firmly believed that the Spiritualism movement was filled with nothing but charlatans was the famous stage magician Harry Houdini. Born Erik Weisz, later going by Harry Weiss, Houdini was a man well versed in the art of deception, as an accomplished illusionist and extraordinary escape artist. His career was based on convincing his audience that his amazing magical acts employed real magick. There were many who believed that he did, in fact, use the assistance of the supernatural to accomplish his stunts (including his elephant-disappearing act). Once, while performing a dangerous stunt in water, something went wrong. Harry almost died, but the spirit of his mother came to him in his moment of need, spoke to him, and ultimately helped him escape what would have been certain death. Afterward, he tried to reach his mother again, enlisting the aid of any Spiritualists he could find. To his dismay, that never happened. Instead, he recognized numerous charlatans and debunked their false claims that they were putting him in touch with his lost loved one. Due to these unfortunate incidents, he found himself on a new path, one of exposing con artists. He became convinced that all Spiritualists were fakes. He did become friends with the Doyles during this phase of his life, but although they were true believers in Spiritualism, Houdini was very convinced that all Spiritualists were charlatans. With the help of hired spies, Houdini discovered that many Spiritualists used the methods of table tipping and fog machines and the power of suggestion to con people into believing they were really communicating with their deceased loved ones.

Many associate the name Allan Kardec with Spiritism, an offshoot of Spiritualism, and he is often credited with being the founder of the discipline. In *The Genesis According to Spiritism*, Kardec stated that Spiritism is "a science that deals with the nature, origin, and destiny of spirits, and their relation with the corporeal world." Allan Kardec was a pen name of a French academic (educator, translator, and author) named Hippolyte Léon Denizard Rivail. Although born a Catholic, he could not help being fascinated by the Spiritualism movement that was going on around the 1850s. As a man of science, he decided to try his hand at communicating with the spirits. He made contact with "Truth," the name given to Rivail by Spirit. In 1857, Allan Kardec wrote a book called *The Spirit's Book*. Readers marveled at the questions that "Truth" was able to answer with regard to the spirits and the spirit realm.

Rivail's Spiritist legacy made it to Spain, where a woman named Amalia Domingo Soler lived. She is well known in the Spanish Spiritist movement. Despite her

Allan Kardec (from *L'Illustration* magazine, 1869)

limited eyesight, she managed to pen *The Revelation* in the city of Alicante. She later wrote *The Spiritist Faith.* The Spanish Spiritists welcomed her to join in their gatherings. On one occasion, Soler read aloud her beautifully written poem titled "To the Memory of Allan Kardec."

In the 1870s, Helena Blavatsky, known by many as Madame Blavatsky, rose to popularity. Unlike those in mainstream Spiritualism, however, she believed that mediums were not contacting the dead. The spirits that were contacted, she asserted, were either the echoes of the deceased or elementals. Blavatsky did practice mediumship, and there were many who believed her to be a fraud. However, she earned a great following.

The year 1875 proved to be an exciting year for Blavatsky, for in that year, she (along with Henry Steel Olcott and William Quan Judge) founded the Theosophical Society. It served as a branch from Spiritualism. Theosophy was the culmination of philosophy, science, and religion. Two years after, Madame Blavatsky published *Isis Unveiled*, a book that detailed her Theosophical belief system and its ties to Sophism, and a favorite book of Albert Einstein's.

Sophism refers to Lady Sophia (Lady Wisdom). She originally came from ancient Greek mythology, but she eventually came to be associated with ancient Hermetic wisdom, and with the Lady Wisdom whom King Solomon wrote about in the *Book of Proverbs* and the *Book of Wisdom*.

For the traditional Christians, Spiritualism was seen as evil. For them, mediumship contacted demons, not spirits of departed loved ones. Even science at the time lashed out at Spiritualism. *Scientific American* magazine dubbed the Fox sisters "Spiritual Knockers from Rochester."

Despite the opposition, Spiritualism thrived! By the late 1800s, there were around eight million believers and practitioners, and there were hundreds of Spiritualist churches/temples. One of the most famous sites related to Spiritualism is in the town of Pomfret, New York. It is called Lily Dale. Lily Dale serves as a pilgrimage site, as it were, for all those interested in Spiritualism, the occult, and the paranormal. It is such a mecca for the occult, with workshops, presentations, and stores; readers/mediums; and other events. Lily Dale prides itself on being a center for the Spiritualist movement's history, a long history going back to the 1800s. This place was incorporated in 1879 as a camp and meeting place for Spiritualists and freethinkers in the first place, so its culture stems from the movement.

In my view, Spiritualism has been at the core of our fundamental understanding of the nature of existence on this plane. It helps us know how to correlate this life with the next. It teaches that the universe is composed by the transmutation of consciousness to matter, of soul to body. Spiritualism gave me the foundation I needed in order to go on to any other mystery school or tradition. My pursuit of Spiritualism proved my grandmother's prediction that I would find the answers I was looking for on my own spiritual path.

MY INTRODUCTION TO SPIRITUALISM

At a very tender age, near when I started primary school, I was exposed to Spiritualism that was very creole in nature, meaning adapted to a new cultural setting or language. I called it Mesa Blanca Criolla. This was my own way of differentiating between the traditional Mesa Blanca (translated as White Table, referring to a working altar for Spiritualists) and our adapted version of it. To me, the Spanish *criolla* (creole) refers to a melting pot of cultures and languages. Cuba's Spiritualism is fused with the African diaspora. It is equivalent to Umbanda, a syncretic faith that began in the nineteenth century, which fused Brazilian Catholic elements with the Orisha. There is a common phrase in Cuban Lucumi traditional teachings that says, "*Ire ilese ocha*." This is a Yoruba phrase that means "Blessings at the foot of the orisha." It's a blessing that I've liked for many years.

I always felt drawn to the paranormal. As an adolescent, though, I became more acutely aware that not all spiritual connection held a positive vibration. Positive or not, spiritual experiences always persisted around me, and I felt the constant presence of an entity acting as an obstruction, a disruptive influence on me. Although grappling with this obstruction seemed a good exercise to enhance my psychic and mediumship abilities, the symptoms of the influence were disturbing. I was often advised that individuals like me, as young conduits of spirit, absorbed energies from our surroundings like sponges. At times, the negative influence I felt—that subversive spirit that frequently made itself known—manifested as internal laughter, a personally audible and quite eerie cackle. During these episodes, I experienced clear and voluminous inflammation, as if my physical body was combating an ailment. The weight of it was beyond explanation. When my grandmother noticed my struggles, she would offer me her rosary, and the pressure would subside. It was then that I realized strongly the need to seek help and find answers for myself.

Cuba's Spiritualism features a chronological order of initiation. Each initiation is a rite of passage for those within the African diaspora. First, there is Palo Mayombe. Second, there is Spiritualism. Third, there is Santeria/Lucumi. The set order is meant to teach the initiate Spiritualism before Lucumi in order to develop one's psychic faculties. I was originally unaware of this prescribed chronological order of initiation, but my circumstances allowed me to go through these initiations in exactly that order with spirit's guidance. I was fascinated to find that out.

Cuban Creole Spiritualists studied the evangelical works of Allan Kardec. The first one was *The Spirit's Book*, the second was *The Medium's Book*, and the third was *The Gospel According to Spiritism*.

My great-grandparents and grandmother experienced the table tappings, the mediums, and the congregations of psychic groups. Cuban Creole Spiritualism was tolerated because of its popularity, but not accepted or endorsed by the Catholic Church, because it was not a part of their official teachings.

BÓVEDA

There were several schools of thought and methods of practice in Cuba when it came to Spiritualism. Some people stood in a circle and worked. The Cuban Creole Spiritualist altar I was brought up with was set up with glasses of water, which was considered a spiritual force for many reasons—its etheric evaporated state being one. This connection was there for us, because as water evaporates, it is like a bridge to connect us with the spirit realm. Water is often used as a divination tool, for scrying. For us, traditional copas, or brandy glasses, were used to represent the *bóveda* (meaning vault, humidor, or crypt).

The setting of the brandy glasses on the white table is very creole, since it is infused with the African diaspora. If seven copas are used, they represent the Seven African Powers. However, if nine copas are used, they represent Oya, the orisha who governs the cemetery, so they refer to the spirits of the dead. The Santísima glass is filled with water first. Then, the other glasses are filled. This reminds me of the Jewish Menorah. The shammash, the maiden candle associated with Shekinah, is the candle in the middle that is lit first. Then the other eight candles are lit. The altar featured representations of one's guardian angel and guides. On it were placed seven to nine glasses plus a big brandy glass, which served as the Santísima, the holy vessel that encompassed the All/primary guardian angel.

THE (GUARDIAN) ANGEL NOVENA

Compañero(a) invisible de mi vida, faro de luz en el mar bravío; que es la existencia. Fiel guardián de los guardianes. Cuando todos se hayan marchado siempre quedarás tú; firme en tu puesto hasta el fin. Quiero despojarme de todas mis impurezas, limpiar mi alma de apetitos y arrojar lejos de mí, mis humanas y muchísimas flaquezas; para así, padre mío, el alma hecha cristalina, mansa a la vez que vigorosa altitud de montaña, bondad de paloma elevar por ti y para ti a Dios; esta sentida plegaria, para que te de cada vez mayor luz, que es progreso; y más misericordia que es premio y es gracia. Compañero(a) invisible de mi vida, juntos hemos recorrer todos el camino en dos planos distintos; 'Las Naves', pero marchando siempre hacia un mismo mundo, en espera de nosotros, el mismo Puerto. Yo hago por ti cuando por ti puede aquí hacerse; y tu haces por mí cuando Desde allá puede Dios para mi lograrse. Hemos sido, somos y seremos el uno para el otro; nací en tu cuna, y estaré a la hora de mi muerte a tu abrigado y protector regazo, y no habrá nada ni nadie, pues es por voluntad divina; que pueda el uno del otro separarnos. Sigue por esos surcos siderales en busca del bien para hacer, de luz para hacer luz; siempre bajo la voluntad de Dios, al que le pido como pan de cada día, que no te prive ni un solo instante de su Santa Bendición.

Novena, Latin for nine, means a special devotional prayer that is traditionally repeated on nine successive days or for nine successive weeks. Here is the English translation David Moore and I have rendered:

Invisible companion of my [entire life], beacon of light in the tumultuous sea, which is the [nature of] existence. Faithful guardian of guardians, when all others have forsaken me, you will always remain steadfast in your duty to the end. Please rid me of all my impurities, cleanse my soul of harmful appetites, and cast off my many human weaknesses. This way, my father, the soul is made crystal clear, meek yet towering at a powerful mountain height. May our pure grace be as a dove in flight, to raise the God nature in you. For you is this heartfelt prayer, so that we may see lighter, which is progress, and more mercy, the reward of grace. Invisible companion of my life, although together we have traveled the path on two different planes, we have always been marching toward the same world waiting for us, the same destination. I do what I can here for you, and you do for me, from there, what God can achieve for me. We have been, are, and will be meant for each other. I was born cradled in your arms, and when I die, I will be held in your warm and protective lap, and there will be nothing or no one that can separate us from each other, because we are together by divine will. Follow the path of the heavens in search of goodness to do, the path of light to make light, always under the will of God, to whom I ask that he does not deprive you for a single moment, as with our daily bread, his Holy Blessing.

Since we are on the subject of guardian angels, I feel it is important that I briefly share my guardian angel story before continuing on with my memories of the Spiritist Temple.

When I was thirteen, I had a profound experience meeting my guardian angel for the first time. I was staying at my grandaunt's house in Miami, Florida, for summer vacation. While lying down in my bed (with the light still on), I beheld my guardian angel standing at the foot of my bed. I saw that he was a monk who carried a staff. He seemed to be one of great elevation.

Saint Barbara and my bóveda, West New York, New Jersey, 1994

At first, I thought he was an African deity. However, I could plainly see that he was actually a Caucasian manifestation. He was very tall, reminding me of my envisioned image of Father Time. I was in awe of his bright silhouette, partially visible and partially in light. He was the most beautiful vision I had ever seen! Fully awake, eyes wide open, I could not only see but also feel his presence. His energy helped me feel the Goddess's divine love and protection for me.

GUIDED BY SPIRIT (ST. MICHAEL THE ARCHANGEL)

I entered a small and simple temple in Union City, New Jersey (the Havana on the Hudson, as it was called), with my best friend, Miguel Angel. It was just a repurposed basement in a tenement building, called San Cristobal de Jesús, La Luz. I was just fifteen years old, and Miguel was only sixteen, and for us it immediately felt like an awakening into a new light. Romualda Garcia, the founder of this establishment, walked up to us right away, and she felt so motherly and inviting. She told me that I had a gift to share, and she assured me that I had come to the right place. I was classified as a newcomer, or seeker, and introduced to others who were new as well. She taught us the protocols expected of newcomers. In time, I would become a full-fledged spirit medium in that congregation. Spiritism, in the form I was exposed to here, resonated with me. It seemed to reflect my "Mesa Blanca Creole" culture from Cuba, a melting pot of elements and practices from all over the world. It was a type of coming home for me, since it would help develop my natural talents in a productive way, and it would give me a taste of spiritual servanthood.

The gatherings were led by Romualda. There was a donation box where people would donate one dollar each for maintenance costs. Maintenance items included traditional resin frankincense on charcoal, herbs (mostly laurel bay leaves), flowers, Florida Water (a citrus and lavender mix with cologne and water), and Kolonia 1800. There was also a German 4711, an aqua cologne. Another favorite was Pompeia Cologne.

On Saturdays, we would have our cleansings. We would start in the afternoon, and our work would end in the evening. When we would gather for rituals, there was designated seating for the public and for the mediums. The public sat in a row of chairs in the back. The mediums sat in the circle of chairs where the White Table was, and there were always two mediums (two women or a man and a woman) who sat at the east or west corners of the table. I sat with the public audience, for I was just a seeker at first. The area, a circle, was closed off to the public via the *cordón* ("cord or rope"). The cordón was composed of tied, colorful *pañuelos* (scarves). The cordón was untied to allow a member of the public access to the circle. Once the public member had been introduced, that public member entered into the circle, and then the cordón would be retied.

One day, my spiritual godmother (Romualda Garcia) decided that I was ready in my development process to join the mediums in their work, and she escorted me to the congregation of approximately thirty-five mediums. I remember feeling intimidated, and that the thirty-five people felt like a crowd of fifty to a hundred to me. There were young adults and elders. Each one was welcoming and inspirational. That day, the mediums were having a session of spiritual cleansings for the public. I had grown accustomed to seeing the proceedings from the back chairs, with the public audience, but from that day on, I was always seated between the mediums. To my left sat my spiritual godmother. To my right sat another female (or sometimes male) medium. Sometimes, during cleansings, personal spiritual disturbances would need to be handled by the mediums as they popped up, but generally we stuck to the cleansings when that was the focus of the day. I remember that the altar faced north, with snifters (brandy glasses) of water, fresh herbs, alum, and flowers with white candles.

I didn't need prompting to participate often. Instead of going with my friends to the nightclubs in NYC, I preferred to spend my time after school and on the weekends with this congregation. I wanted to develop my psychic abilities, part of my mediumship development. It was remarkable that I was allowed to assist in the cleansings and consultations with clients for four years at such a young age—such tasks were generally reserved for adult mediums, but I took to it like a fish to water and found a lot of fulfillment helping people in this way.

Two days of the week were devoted to psychic consultations with remedies prescribed for the individuals, having them do their homework of developing an altar, meditation, prayers (or spells), and special types of baths. This regular practice paved the way for us to decipher and come up with a root system for the analysis of spiritual obstructions and virtues. The development process was, and still is, a lifetime of dedication and discipline. Every mystery school, including Spiritism, has some sort of process of connecting to and becoming aware of and functional with a higher consciousness, which I always equated to our soul.

Romualda Garcia was the primary source of my training. She believed in me; she saw a special light in me, even though I was still so young. She was always very accurate in her consultations (*consultas*). She was gifted with clairsentience, clairaudience, and clairvoyance. She was also a Palera, a priestess of the same Congo religion I

My godmother, Romualda Garcia, and I

was exposed to years earlier by René. Romualda saw in me the potential to become who I am today with reverence and humility. She also foresaw that I would become a priest for the people. I remember she said to me that she saw me, in my future, as a distinguished gentleman in a suit, with salt-and-pepper hair, with glasses, traveling as a special representative and staying in hotels here and there. And Romualda was ultimately responsible for organizing my *bóveda spiritual*, teaching me how to concentrate in meditative exercises, and helping me build my relationship with my spirit guides and guardian angel.

During this development process, I saw the aforementioned guardian angel again. Romualda was there with me the whole time, and she guided me on the meditative journey. I met my guardian angel more formally here in the higher state of consciousness, the deep meditative state. In it, I saw my guardian angel walking with his staff onto a boat that resembled a canoe, or pirogue, and he remained standing, still gripping his staff, while the boat drifted through the water of a narrow river or stream. Eventually, I watched him exit the boat and walk on the other side. After this, in my mind's eye, I saw the novice (the image Raul had drawn for me). I always had religious entities within my spiritual paradigm. I knew I was an old soul. (According to Michael Pendragon, I am about 250,000 years old. Michael, an accomplished astrologer from Salem, known throughout Massachusetts, was an original member of Black Doves of Isis, with Laurie Cabot.) Following the novice, some powerful and higher-vibrational entities revealed themselves to me.

To this day, I miss those Spiritist gatherings. They offered warmth, humility, servanthood, and spiritual development for all. Above all, this community served as a spiritual refuge for those in need. There were many different people who sought relief there, including those of Hispanic, Italian, Irish, and German backgrounds. Spirit would always have accurate results for them, whether positive or not. Truth prevailed. It was very gratifying to be a part of that! It had heart, and it was so sincere and kind.

I once helped a married (but separated) man who wanted to win back the good graces of his wife. As I recall, she had beautiful hazel eyes and jet-black hair (like Elizabeth Taylor). She actually modeled with me once at the legendary Studio 54 in New York City (although she wasn't a professional model, at that time I was modeling regularly for Click Model Management in Manhattan). The man hoped they would have a chance to get back together. However, I was honored to help them come to a healthy conclusion to their marriage—what they really needed. In helping them find closure, I met his family and his ex-wife's family. They were Cuban Americans from Summerset, New Jersey. I made friends with all of them.

There was one particular sister in this family who was said to be suffering from psychological trauma. Psychiatric professionals had failed to properly diagnose her. The family asked me if her problem was spiritual. I sensed that was the case, and that she needed the help of the temple. With assistance from the Spiritist community, she finally found what she needed. After the first session at the temple, she expressed genuine, heartfelt relief. She was psychologically sound. Her problem turned out to be a "character enamorado" (a misguided spirit, without light, who was in limbo and had gravitated to the strong virgin energy). I felt great that I had accurately listened to Spirit and took her to the temple, and she got properly assessed and cleansed by the Great Mother. I loved making such a difference!

After a hiatus, I came back to the temple at the age of nineteen. Romualda was delighted that I had returned. She declared that I was totally prepared to have my crowning, because I was in tune with my guardian angel and spiritual guides, my spiritual ability had been heightened, and I had mastered the Spiritist work for the good of all.

Soon thereafter, the big day had arrived. Crowning is done to help solidify or affirm/identify the commissions—*la commisiones*—which are composed of spirit guides, to work with in the future. It is a formal firming of the contract with these spirits. There was a ceremony consisting of thirty to forty mediums in a circle. I wore poor, disposable clothing but had fine clothes with me, as instructed. It was a private affair; the only ones invited were those close to me. They were all excited for me! And they marveled that a nineteen-year-old boy would become the youngest of them to be crowned thus far.

Although technically an adult at that age, I was directed to sit on the floor, as a child would, in a lotus position. Romualda opened the ceremony. After that, there was the typical protocol of the introduction of prayers and novenas. Then, each medium journeyed into a higher state of consciousness, one wherein psychic abilities were fully opened, seeking visions about me. Then each one wrote what they had seen, using pad and pencil. After all of this was done, each medium shared with me what they had written down.

Then the moment came for me to reach my own meditative state of higher consciousness. During this time, all of my guides (in order from lower to higher vibrations) came to me. The last of these was my prominent guardian angel. My ancestors and my sister (as she would have been) also appeared. All of these important spirits were appearing as they needed to for me, mostly because the mediums had fashioned a sacred circle portal. Only the correct entities were allowed in the circle (those with good intentions). Each spirit being granted me a blessing of higher power when he/she manifested. It was a joyous occasion!

In the next part of the ceremony, my shanty clothing was ripped and shredded (the ripping of the clothing was a shedding of the past and being born again). Then I went into a private room and changed into the celebratory ensemble to represent the new beginning in finery for my coronation! A lot more cleansing was done at this time. There was also singing. Together, the mediums made up a unified vibrational pool. They expertly raised the vibrations while I remained in the center of the circle. I was blessed in the cone of power that was given me.

Afterward, some of the mediums presented me with gifts. Then, there was a celebration of Spanish and Cuban cuisine. It was lovely! Through my crowning (a metaphor of the unification of the spiritual paradigm), I had reached the highest level of enlightenment available in this mystery school. It was my final rite of passage in the Spiritist community.

Iku lobi Ocha—Without spirit, there is no Santo. Iré Elese Ocha—Blessings will come at the feet of the Orisha.

—Alexander Cabot

ABORU ABOYE ABOISE

I had the privilege of meeting and interviewing Reverend Alexander Cabot, High Priest in the Cabot Tradition of Witchcraft, with my cohost, Teresa Sliwinski, the Slavic Witch, on our show *Ancestral Eyes* in 2020. It can be found recorded as season 1, episode 26. We were both impressed with Reverend Cabot's knowledge and fascinating life journey through various spiritual belief systems, including Afro-Cuban systems such as Palo Mayombe and Regla de Ocha / Ifá / Lucumi. I could relate in many ways, since both Alexander and I are sons of Cuban mothers with some French ancestry. Looking at the makeup of his family's religious and spiritual traditions, I see many parallels to my own spiritual journey that culminated in my becoming a Babalawo (Ifá Priest). In my family, there were also Freemasons, Spiritists, Paleros (Tatas and Yayas), Santeros (Iyalorisas and Babalorisas), and Babalawos. Meeting Alexander, there was an instant spiritual brotherly bond of shared experiences and traditions.

What stood out most for me is Alexander's down-to-earth personality, his polite and genuine nature, and his broad spiritual experience "in the trenches" coming up and being exposed to and initiated into many of our Cuban traditions. I was honored when he asked for my endorsement or contribution. I was happy to help edit and recall aspects of one of the Cuban religious traditions he belonged to in New York; namely, Regla de Ocha (or Ifá). This allowed us to reminisce and compare notes in a spirit of humility and genuine scholarly interest, in order to present a valuable overview and understanding of this belief system. Its roots come from western Nigeria, from the Yoruba people, the Benin Republic (Fon-Gbe), Togo (Ewe), and Ghana (Ewe/Akan). It was brought with slaves during the transatlantic slave holocaust, and it survived centuries in the widespread diaspora in Cuba, Brazil, the US, Haiti, and other nations, ultimately becoming the sixth-largest belief system in the world. Frankly, I was fascinated at the fact that he had become a High Priest in the Cabot Tradition, a duty for which he has a natural spiritual gift, and a great deal of history and experience to pull from. He is well respected and loved by his fellow Cabots, and he is a worthy ambassador and spokesperson for that tradition. I wish him every success in this book effort, and in all of his future endeavors. I am incredibly grateful to his wonderful publisher for their interest and promotion of our spiritual traditions, and for their support of Alexander.

Many blessings. Ire bogbo. Aśe-o.

Baba Baudry is cofounder and producer for *Ancestral Eyes*, a podcast show, and is president and cofounder at Consejo Cultural Yorùbá de Canada. He contributed some wonderful details to the following chapter, especially to a few pataki.

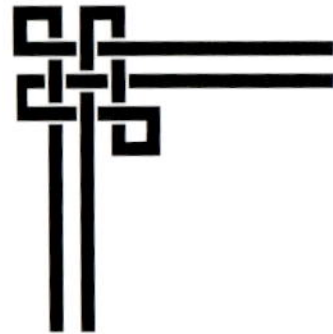

CHAPTER 6
LUCUMI

I have always said that religion is all man-made, and that it results from our interpretation of spirituality. My early environment and culture steeped me in religious systems that came from the African diaspora. One of the most well known, and one of the first I encountered, was Santeria. Santeria is a syncretic spiritual practice. "Santeria" has its root in "santo," which is the Spanish word for "saint." It fuses the faith of those from a tribe of Yoruba people from western Nigeria, as well as the Fon/Ewe people of the modern Republic of Benin, with Roman Catholicism, as a result of the African slaves being forced to accept Catholicism. Through syncretism, the enslaved Yoruba people were able to preserve their heritage and traditions, and to export their religion out into the world at large. As a little boy in a Cuban American community, with a Catholic background and magickal family history, I was always fascinated with people who were identified as Santeros or Santeras. I was fascinated by the practice and aesthetics of the tradition of Santeria we called Lucumi.

The Yoruba people made up a good percentage of the captured Nigerians trafficked through Cuba in its financial heyday. Cuba was called "key of the Gulf," and traders of all sorts filled its ports. Havana was the main hub of this activity, since it was the metropolis of the Caribbean. Although some accounts say that the church helped create it, the official stance of the Catholic Church is that it does not condone the practice of Santeria. Some say it originated in Africa, due to the efforts of monks to create a middle ground and gain the people. However, my understanding of the history is that it came to North America from the Cuban African diaspora, first during the migration from Cuba between the 1940s and 1950s and then in a second wave from the 1960s through the 1980s. The Orisha are seen as blessed spirits who represent deified forces of nature that encompass the five Yoruba elements: fire, water, air, earth, and metal. Orisha are very much like the Hebrew concept of angels, tasked with certain responsibilities or areas of expertise in the vicinity of the earth. Santeria has syncretized the Orisha with some of the Catholic saints (human ancestors the church declared to be saints).

Santeria became known as Regla de Ocha when it was established in Cuba, and later it was colloquialized as Lucumi. There are marked differences between Ifá (the Yoruba mother tradition) and Regla de Ocha, but the core ideas remain very much the same.

Orúnmila is the oracle. He is also called Ifá, which is the name of the original African tradition, and since he provides the information for all divinations, and that information is used as the basis for all decisions in life, he is considered the head of the practice. Prescribed sacrifices, spiritual cures, medicines, and much more all come from Ifá, or Orúnmila. Regla de Ocha, a more local tradition that did originally come from Ifá, was heavily present in Cuba for a long time, but eventually the mother tradition was also present in its original glory.

There has been a lot of rivalry between the original African tradition and the creole tradition that was better rooted in Cuba, but in my view they always should have worked together. Often, one will say they should be consulted first, and the other will reciprocate the opposing view. Sometimes, it has been an actual battle between the Oriaté and the Babalawo, between Regla de Ocha and Ifá, and I wish they would get along better. Their practices are just as valid, and strongly akin to each other through their shared history. Lucumi was the local Creole name given it, so that term is indigenous to Cuba. I was taught that Lucumi translates to "friendship" by my Oriaté.

To the practitioners of Lucumi, the Catholic God corresponds to their ultimate deity, known as Olodumare. Jesus is often syncretized with Olofi ("He who governs or owns the palace"), the conduit between heaven and earth. In my thoughts, Olofi is a personification of God's prana, or breath energy. In Lucumi tradition, we call this breath of life Aché. I learned from my Oriaté that there are legends about the orisha, stories called Patakí. The traditional 256-story set makes up the mythology of the Yoruba people, and the core of understanding for practitioners.

IN THE BEGINNING

Akamara, a primal form of Olodumare, was all that existed in the beginning. His active spirit, Olofi, sometimes syncretized with the Holy Spirit of Christianity, carried out his creative wishes as he fashioned the universe. The center of the earth was created with its own spirit, then the mass of deep waters, which were personified by Olokun. From those depths, up came the upper waters and lands. Yemaya gave birth to all the other orisha. The first orisha to touch the land was "Oduduwa/Odúwa" (at least that's how I remember the name pronounced), considered by some in Cuba to be a path of Obatala, as is the case with my Oriaté, so that is what I was taught. He is known to be as soft as cotton, silent and dark, poised between the living and the dead. All natural materials and forces were controlled by certain orisha, assigned to their tasks, and given their dominions. That is the way Olodumare created order. All things were governed, instructed, and watched. Interacting with creation, with nature itself, therefore, requires humans to honor and respect and communicate with those spirits.

Elegua was created to be the past, present, and future; he is the beginning and the end. Elegua is the gatekeeper, warrior angel, and guardian of roads. He is syncretized with San Antonio de Padua, and also with Santo Niño de Atocha (a Christ child image from Toledo, Spain). He must be placed with all other orisha in order to honor them. He was associated with a coconut, because Olodumare told him, "You will be like the coconut, dirty on the outside and clean on the inside." The Yoruba equivalent is Eshu, or Eśu. One path of Elegua, the youngest, is Eśu Alaroye. This avatar sits behind every practitioner's door to guard it. Sometimes a representation of his head is placed at the door. He is a warrior/guardian of homes and comes to Earth to play with children, playing tricks at crossroads. He is related to money and financial luck, betting, and gambling. Several paths of Eśu also oversee the dead and communication with them, as well as being a messenger to the powerful Iyami Osooronga (great mothers, considered the witches).

Elegua, also called Echu, in my home

Here is a pataki according to a good friend of mine, who is a Babalawo, about two such paths of Eśu, who are guardians of the cemetery: Eśu Obakaleto and Eśu Boru.

Yemaya, in charge of the cemetery, left Oya in her stead. She tricked Oya, leaving her enslaved at the cemetery gate, and went to live in the sea. Oya, while enslaved, went to live with Obakaleto, who was the foreman of the Egun, and he told her that he would always defend her. He told her that he was an Eśu that, at night, looked after the graves, all covered with *mariwó* (dried palm fronds), with a lamp in hand, and by day he lives guarding the cemetery gate and that he eats everything humans throw away at the door of Iku's house.

DIVINATION

Divination by the Babalawos in Cuba is done with the epuele chain, composed of eight ikin seeds with a metal chain. However, for Lucumi practitioners, most basic divinations are performed using coconut shell pieces. Simple questions are asked and answered with these pieces of shell, but for divination of more-serious issues, especially those directly involving the orisha, they use the "mouth of the orisha," a set of twenty-one cowrie shells. People consult them to learn matters of love, career, spiritual activities, and other important areas of their lives. These divinations are a result of communication with Orúnmila, the keeper of all occult knowledge.

Orúnmila wasn't always the keeper of knowledge. At first, Ifá (knowledge of all things) was given to Chango. To make a long story short, he didn't like the responsibility, so he looked for a more serious person to handle the duty with honor. He chose Orúnmila, but he promised to help if he got into trouble. It is that legacy that created the requirement that whenever Ifá is given to an initiate, Chango must be present.

Orúnmila is likened to King Solomon's spirit of Wisdom. It was Orúnmila who worked with Obatala, the father and head of all Orisha on Earth, who dresses in and emanates the color white, to create firm ground on Earth. Not long afterward, Olofi tasked Obatala with creating female and male humans out of clay. Olofi told Obatala to leave the clay humans on the ground so the sun could dry them out.

The Lucumi revere St. Francis of Assisi as the equivalent to the Orisha Orúnmila. In her book *Santeria: The Religion*, Migene González-Wippler says that "Orúnmila's day is celebrated on October 4, the day of Saint Francis in the Catholic Church. On that day the Babalawo's 'godchildren,' the ones who have received initiations from him, come to his house to pay their respects to Orúnmila. They must bring with them two coconuts, a name, two white candles, and a derecho (offering) of $1.05 or whatever they wish to give."

MY DANCE WITH OTHER IMPORTANT ORISHA

Olokun (sometimes pictured as a mermaid, but actually Olokun's appearance is a mystery and often is seen as hermaphrodite) is the depths of the abyss and deepest mysteries. Olokun is the depths of the ocean. Yemaya rises from Olokun. Yemaya surfaces on the waters of the ocean, and she gives birth to all of the other Orisha. Yemaya is syncretized with La Virgen de Regla (one of the forms of the Virgin Mary). She is connected with the River Ogun, and I like to honor her with the phrase "Omio Yemaya." Her feast day is September 7, and she is strongly associated with the number seven.

Ayagunna is important to me, since this is a specific "path" of Obatala, or avatar. He is uncommon to learn about, and he wears white clothing with a red sash and is armed with an Arabian sword, a scimitar. For that reason, he sometimes is mistaken for being Chango, who bears the same colors. His pataki, or story, is that he is the youngest avatar of Obatala. He is a guide and a father to me, and I have often seen him dressed similarly to traditional Arab clothing, mounted on his white stallion, when I have had visions of him. He is an elegant warrior of nature, very powerful and imposing visually. He is known for having spread gunpowder throughout the world, following orders from Olodumare. Once, when he appeared to me, he introduced himself as Ayagunna Leibo, meaning "ferocious dog," he said, since he is the warrior of the universe. He enforces the laws of Olofi. He is known for saying, "Father, without conflict, there can be no progress." Similarly, many people say, "Without war, there is no peace." Obatala is known for being peaceful and calm, but even his patience has limits, and when he sees the futility of kindly asking and directing people to follow the laws of Olofi, and he puts his foot down to enforce what must be, Ayagunna creates peace by swift and decisive military actions, when they are needed.

My first encounter with Ayagunna was a drumming ceremony, called Tambor de Fundamento. There are two main types of sacred drumming practiced in the Lucumi tradition, the güiro and tambor de fundamento. The latter is considered the most holy drumming to the Orisha. The drummers actually have a special organized fraternity, with their own rites of passage, and they consecrate their drums and perform sacred and secret rites that result in their drums having spirits of their own, living spirits that reside within the drums. This occurred in Union City, New Jersey, with a group of Santeros and Santeras, celebrating the anniversary of someone's initiation. Also, there was a powerful effect of community present. Everyone had their part to play, whether plucking a bird or decorating the area, and they were all lending their energies to the event.

We began with the customary Oro a Eggún, which is how we began the festivities, honoring the spirits of our ancestors. These can be blood relatives or others we were close to like family, or to whom we had a strong spiritual connection. We then sacrificed a boar, removing its head and cleaning it properly to use in the making of a consommé, to make the base of a stew called a Cuban ajiaco. Lots of vegetables and starches were then added, making a great traditional dish for us to enjoy later. Cascarilla, made from eggshells laid out in the sun and then pulverized, was used to mark the ground in a semicircular area around the special altar/shrine that we had set up. It was grand, and the energies danced through the air as we got more and more into the mood. Various verses were recited, and under the guidance of an Oriaté, we performed several incantations together. Once underway, the festivities continued as we proceeded into the Great Hall. Three drummers were present, and the dancers bowed and paid respect to the drums (they bowed and kissed the drums, out of respect for the spirit of the drum, called *aña*) as they were beginning their dance. Right then, for the first time, I saw someone ridden (which is what we call being possessed) by Ayagunna, an Oriaté, a Chief High Priest of Lucumi. I perceived the duality of the two personalities, as he danced in a circular motion.

He seemed to be blessing everyone as he was possessed. It was a graceful dance, enlightened and loving, while fiercely protective of all. He wasn't there to fight, so the movements weren't so much warlike as one may expect, but he was joining in our festivities. He embraced several people, including me! It was electrifying and beautiful. My emotions spiraled. I felt accepted and blessed. I remember his eyes were wide open, even to the point of bulging out, with dilated pupils. It was obvious that the spirit had taken over the man. The behavior and the movement were completely different. I knew the embrace was from the entity that was "riding" him, not the man. Emotion is not primitive. Emotion is divine. I was overwhelmed with strong emotion, and I knew I was touching the sacred. Many people mistake emotion for weakness, but it is the opposite—emotion creates the strongest magick, it explodes throughout the universe, and it is how all things exist. These special experiences of possession serve more purpose than merely to spread blessings. They serve an informative function, giving messages to those who are invited.

I was once given the task of helping someone to receive Babalú Ayé (in Yoruba, it is Obalúwayé). Desi Arnaz popularized the Cuban song called "Babalu," originally written by Margarita Lecuona, about this orisha. Babalú Ayé is associated with healing in all aspects, the elderly, and the infirm. I was given a special necklace, beaded with brown and white with blue stripes and black accents, his colors. He is close to the spirit of death, since he is a healer and caretaker for the elderly, for those who are soon to die, and who watches over the homeless. He is associated with heat, believed to cause fevers in order to expel diseases, and is syncretized with Saint Lazarus, who was a leper and who was resurrected. Babalú Ayé is often seen as a figure hobbled by disease, since he carries the weight of disease for all mankind. We did the ritual in the heat of the day, in his honor, and it was quiet and peaceful. I remember that we focused all on the ground, since he dwells there, and we had to walk slowly. We were inside the Great Hall, with very few small candles. It was a silent and dark event, and an ominous feeling flowed throughout the space. I was left with a feeling of humility and a feeling of kindness and charity toward humanity.

One of the most important Orisha has always been Ochun, a river goddess who is said to be the youngest of the Orisha. Ochun Yalorde, or Queen Ochun, is a popular title for her. In the pataki about her that I am familiar with, the earth was going to be destroyed, according to a message sent via Olofi. All the orisha were trying to reach Olodumare, but he would not grant an audience or listen to anyone. Ochun transformed herself into a vulture, and she was able to get to the height of Olodumare's throne. She pleaded for the salvation of humanity, and he did not destroy the world. Although she was the youngest of them all, she was honored as Ochun Yalorde, the queen. Oba is the true Lady of Love, senior wife of Shango, and she gave Ochun the key to love in order to honor her. In that way, Ochun was seen as the successor of Oba, the new Goddess of Love. No wonder she was so important! Savior of humanity and keeper of love, she is venerated worldwide.

Although, on the surface, it is easy to recognize saintly devotion (along with devotion to Christ and his blessed mother Mary), it is important to note that Santeria is a private and oral-tradition practice, where each priest's or priestess's home is their temple. Much of what is practiced involves rituals that I was privately taught. Not much has been written about this tradition, but my spirit's journey, led by the Goddess, did tread the path of Santeria. And some of my spirit guides who revealed themselves to me during my journey as an initiate of Santeria (Lucumi) are still with me.

In my own personal practice, I offer sacrifices of cigars, incense, and other gifts to the Orisha, and in the past I have offered blood sacrifices, where the animal is honored and then consumed. However, in my daily practice, I choose not to give such offerings unless absolutely necessary. I would like to point out that in the Bible, blood is mentioned more than the word "God." Blood sacrifice has been an important component to ritual workings in every religion since the dawn of time as we know it, according to the evidence we seem to have. Blood is the essence of life. All of us carry this lifeforce in our blood. It is used in almost every ancient tradition, and Lucumi is not an exception.

When I place the representation of the Orisha in places of honor in my home, I am careful not to put them all in one place. It is important to honor each Orisha separately, in different areas. There are some Orisha that can be honored together. Most notably, Elegua must be honored with everyone, because he is the gatekeeper. Although each one is connected to Olodumare, not all of them get along. In regard to Yemaya, I offer her flowers and water with añil (a blue dye we used to get from certain plants of the Indigofera

I offer candy, money, cigars, and more.

family). People have long used bluing (this dye) to make their white laundry look whiter. Interestingly, this dye and its history were brought to North America from Africa. In her book *Indigo: In Search of the Color That Seduced the World*, Catherine E. McKinley indicates that the slave trade significantly influenced the indigo craze in the 1700s. In the article "The Devil's Blue Dye: Indigo and Slavery," Jean M. West states that indigo cloth was dyed by Yoruba women. Also, in the same article, "laundry bluing (which made white fabrics appear whiter)" was said to have come out of the same indigo trade.

When I was sixteen, a Santero told me that I was a child of Yemaya, because he had beheld me in a vision. I appeared as a little Caucasian boy who was peeking under the skirt of La Madama (a spiritual guide that I have who represents Yemaya). I thanked him for confirming that I am Yemaya's child.

As I write this, I am sitting in my altar room looking at an amazing image of Yemaya on the wall above my altar. It is a print of a Brazilian painting. Even though it's not a Cuban image, it is special because it was given to me when I was a young boy. Brazil has their own set of African diaspora traditions, most notably Candomble and Umbanda. The original painting was done during the Portuguese colonial era. The plan for the painting was for it to represent Isis, but the Afro-Brazilian religious culture influenced the painter, who then portrayed her as a Caucasian version of Yemaya. In Brazil, the image has become extremely popular, even iconic, as a representation of Yemaya. The portrait features a woman with long, dark hair. She is crowned with pearls and a starfish, and she is wearing a long, ghostly bluish-white dress. She is walking on the ocean waters at night. For Cubans, the image seems to go back further in the history of the world, to the mysterious depths of the ocean, Olokun. To me, the painting is an image of my Goddess, and I smile in wonder as I gaze upon it regularly.

Yemaya celebration, Miami, Florida, 1993

In some lineages in Cuba, one of the paths, or avatars, of Yemaya is Nana Burukú. She is syncretized with Santa Ana. She is considered to be the great-grandmother to all orisha, an advocate for women's rights, a protector of children, saving those who are abused, a bringer of peace, and a fighter for good causes. She is wisdom and strength to me, and when I am in her presence, I feel magick and protection, comforted as if I am her grandchild. She presides over the rivers, lagoons, and swamps. She is connected with the magick of the moon. Her pataki that was passed to me states that she was confrontational and even abusive to Ogun, her husband by arrangement, and then there's a very different story, wherein she leaves Ogun, and he takes away all metals from her. "As long as the earth is alive, you will use wood. I extract from you all metal." She had to use only bamboo knives, for instance, and her devotees couldn't use metal in her rites. Some believe she is the one who originated the menstrual cycle for

My painting of Yemaya

women, to cleanse their sacred vessels. Blood sacrifices to her are done knowing that she consumes the spirit of the animal, and unlike the others, she ignores the blood, which just returns to the earth. She must be received with Babalú Ayé.

PATH TO PRIESTHOOD

I later embarked on my spiritual journey to become a santero when I was twenty-three years old, for it was at that age that La Madama revealed herself to me in a dream, an Afro-Caribbean spiritual guide dressed in blue and white, giving me the Olokun in *tinaja de barro*, a clay vessel used by slaves to hide their Orisha inside. (Sometimes they would take and use soup tureens from their masters' hutches for this purpose, and people can buy soup tureens from botánicas to place their orisha in to this day.) She told me I would be receiving all of this soon. This revelation confirmed what I had innately knew, that my most important personal spiritual entity was La Madama. Other people, Spiritualists and those of other spiritual paths, also confirmed this fact.

Through the help of various people, I met the man for whom I would apprentice. I recognized him as an Oriaté, a chief high priest. My Oriaté knew that I was coming and knew that I would be his apprentice. He knew because it was mentioned that this young man with a Roman feature profile would come into his life for him to guide and lead him onto the path of Regla de Ocha. I was able to learn all the rites of passage within Regla de Ocha. Although, as with all communities, there was a lot of political interaction, inflated egos, and differences of opinion, which is human nature; that is not my preferred focus. Spiritual matters are most important to me. I stayed out of politics and tried to avoid bumping my head on egos.

The Oriaté provided me with guidance, training, and an assortment of tools and materials to work with, which normally would come at a premium cost. Because he had foreseen that I was meant to be his apprentice and have them, all of this was given freely to me, a special honor that I'm grateful for. My first involvement with him was assisting him with several of his *itutos* (the funeral rites for Santeros and Santeras). I remember doing a lot of the itutos and ochas in the Bronx, Brooklyn, and New Jersey. We also did cleansings, and I assisted him in more major workings, such as giving certain orisha to initiates.

Ogun and Ochosi, two of the three warriors who are usually together

Initiation is given when it is needed, and when the recipient is ready. It is said that without spirit, there is no santo. The orisha represent forces of nature, so when the initiate receives their own "guardian angel," whom they belong to, it's not truly a legendary personality or archetype they receive, but the spirit of the natural forces they need to protect or guide them. A partnership is formed between the initiate's higher self and the orisha spirit.

My Oriaté was one of the good people who came from the Mariel boat lift, a mass emigration of Cubans who traveled from Cuba's Mariel Harbor to the USA. Castro saw the opportunity to sneak in among them a hoard of prisoners, mentally ill, and even homosexual people (considered deviants by Castro just for their orientation), in an effort to "cleanse" Cuba of its riffraff. The resulting crowd was rife with murderers, thieves, rapists, insane criminals, et al., but also intermingled in that crowd were the original composition of political dissidents, including upper-class families, skilled tradesmen, and laborers.

He introduced me to a community in Manhattan that had a temple in Chelsea. It was an industrial warehouse that had been converted into a Santeria temple. It was formed by Jewish American practitioners. Many ceremonies were conducted there. The lead Jewish founder had initiated practitioners for over ten years at that time. I was impressed by how well managed the temple was, and how properly it was set up. It thrilled me that my native culture's religion was evolving to include people of other cultural backgrounds.

We often traveled to Miami, where a lot of the ceremonies would be performed. During this time, I gained a lot of the experience and exposure I needed to practice the system. In Miami, I was given many of my initiatory rites. I left the Lucumi community to focus on college and my career for a while. Sadly, I received the news that my dear Oriaté passed away, and I was left with the memories and knowledge he passed to me to honor him with.

Shortly after I graduated from college, my heart was guided by my Goddess toward the study and practice of Wicca.

As we honor our elders, we honor ourselves.

—Alexander Cabot

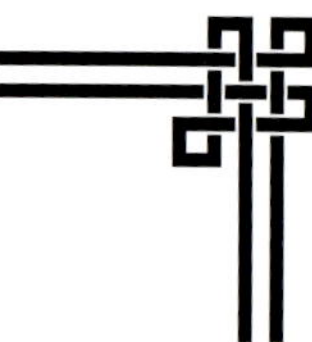

CHAPTER 7
THE MAGICKAL CHILDE

I have a spirit guide who is a crone, an old British traditional crone. She manifested herself to me when I was young. It was due to her guidance that I, at the tender age of eleven, was drawn to the Tarot, Aleister Crowley, and British Traditional Witchcraft. (At a later date, mediums confirmed the crone's presence in my life.)

As a young boy, in 1979, I was in search of myself and the Old Religion. However, I was also what was known as an original Club Kid, part of a subculture of the New York City nightlife. (Club Kids became a popular term in the 1990s, but I was involved with the beginning of the trend in the early '80s.) One day, while I was heading in the direction of the Danceteria, a nightclub which was located on West 21st Street, for my first Madonna performance, I happened upon the Magickal Childe. At the entrance of this occult shop, I was struck with keen anticipation and wonder! Years later, I would be frequenting the Limelight club on the same street, and the Magickal Childe became my main stomping ground and hangout.

The Virgo in me immediately noticed that the shop appeared dusty, old, and unkempt. It reminded me of a place that one might encounter in a creepy, scary house, if it weren't for the conveniently placed Coca Cola vending machine next to the door. On the ceiling, there was a flying devil hanging with bat wings and Pan legs. Its eyes popped out like black olives. It was like something out of the *Twilight Zone*! There was a movie with Nicolas Cage, called *Vampire Kiss*, where his character enters into the Magickal Childe and walks up to the counter. A truly striking scene. It made a deep impression immediately.

In unison with my initiatory take of the occult store, I was hit with something powerful . . . an alluring smell! It was an enchanting incense called Gloria's Tears. As I

Magickal Childe, Chelsea, New York City

inhaled the incense, I was instantly under the spell of Herman Slater (owner of the Magickal Childe), Eddie Buczynski, Lady Rhea, Carol Buzone, and Lady Rhiannon. All of these people were key movers and shakers within the occult and Wiccan community. They would become pioneers of what would be New York Wica, Welsh Traditionalists, and the Minoan Brotherhood and Sisterhood. Somehow, all of this destiny was wrapped up in Gloria's Tears for me. Since I was initiated with it in powdered form, every time I catch the scent of it, I am transported back into the Magickal Childe in my youth.

I was in total awe of the mix of bohemian, downtown grassroots culture of New York City with the occultism of Slater's shop. The Magickal Childe was the epicenter of the occult sciences, frequented by famous New York personalities such as Deborah Harry, Dan Aykroyd, Chris Stein (of the band Blondie), Yoko Ono, and John Lennon. The shop even received regular phone orders from Agnes Moorehead (of the famous television show *Bewitched*). Moorehead was a practicing Alexandrian witch, who had an account with the Magickal Childe.

When I visited the store, I delighted in seeing "all the accoutrements" (as Herman used to say). These "accoutrements" included an assortment of occult items, such as books, candles, incense, statues, ritual robes, and music cassette tapes. The store had items related to Hinduism, Buddhism, Crowley's Thelema, menorahs, and mezuzahs. No notable shop would be complete without T-shirts, of course, so Magickal Childe shirts were sold there as well.

The Magickal Childe epitomized what occultism was in New York City. It was a store that housed an amalgamation of all types of practices and beliefs, from the Abrahamic faiths all the way to Satanism. Naturally, I was drawn to the store's occult flavor. I enjoyed several books, including *The Facts of Witchcraft* by Eddie Buczynski (published by Herman Slater), a book I bought there and still have as of this printing. I also enjoyed Herman Slater's *Magickal Formularies I and II*. Herman Slater's other notable works were *Pagan Rituals III: Outer Court Training Coven* and *Pioneer Occultist* (The Magickal Childe) *Part I and Part II of Behutet: Modern Thelemic Magick and Culture*.

In order to appreciate Slater's most famous book, *Necronomicon* (one of my personal favorites), one must first consider its background history. It all began with the fictional book *Necronomicon* (also referred to as the *Book of the Dead*) by the literary horror fiction genius H. P. Lovecraft which was referred to in some of Lovecraft's short stories, beginning with "The Hound." Later, in the 1970s, an Eastern Orthodox priest, Peter Levenda (publicly known as Simon), published his book titled *Necronomicon*. Simon claimed to have been the editor (not the original author of the grimoire). He claimed to have found the original text that Lovecraft mentioned in his short stories.

In 1977, Herman Slater, with his magickal training and knowledge, was able to produce New York City's own grimoire that was based on Lovecraft's *Necronomicon*. He did this with the aid of Malcolm Mills, Cyndi, and Simon. Unlike in the fictious grimoire, Slater's rendition of the *Necronomicon* brought the masses a real, tangible, living force of magick. I remember seeing the ad for the book. It stated that there were a total of 666 leather-bound copies. The number 666 was used as a reference to the biblical number of the beast, of course, mentioned in Revelation. Some were gilded; others were editions embossed with silver. They were once sold at Herman's shop. My cousin bought a silver copy of the *Necronomicon* for me from the ad. Slater's *Necronomicon* version inspired many people to believe that the grimoire was real, not based in fiction as many literary critics have proposed. Later, in 1993, the occult classic film *Necronomicon* was released. Despite the fact that it was not a well-made movie, the fascination for the grimoire continued.

Herman Slater not only was the author of these fabulous books and the owner of the Magickal Childe but also was a high priest of the Welsh Tradition, and I admired and respected him. As it turned out, he took a liking to me from the start as well. I vividly recall when I took the liberty of reading books by the bookshelves. Other kids would see what I was doing, and they would follow suit. However, Slater would scream at them (not me), saying, "What do you think, this is, the New York City Public Library? Get out! Buy the book or get the fuck out!" I chuckle as I recall the sign Slater posted in the shop. It read "Buy or Bye." He had no issues with those who were true seekers or genuine customers (or both). Herman knew that I was both. Plus, he appreciated the fact that I was respectful when I perused through the books and Tarot decks. Slater was known as "Horrible Herman." In fact, there were many times when people would refer to him as Gargamel, from the famous 1980s animated television show *The Smurfs*. However gruff his exterior, he was not really a mean person. Herman did enjoy those who frequented the Magickal Childe. But after about five minutes or so, he would size up the people, kids or not, and act accordingly.

It was at the Magickal Childe that I discovered Rolla Nordic, born Murielle Doris Berulfsen. I was deeply impressed by her book *Tarot Shows the Way* and her Rolla Nordic Tarot deck. I was excited to learn that Nordic was a great witch during that time period in New York City. Sadly, she is an Elder of the Craft who has largely been forgotten. Look her up and honor her.

I'm holding *Behutet* with Herman Slater on the cover, at Magickal Childe

Another famous witch I have always admired was Sybil Leek. Back in 2002, the British Broadcasting Company dubbed her "Britain's most famous witch." I took great joy in reading the following books (sold in the Magickal Childe) by Sybil: *The Sybil Leek's Astrological Guide to Successful Everyday Living*, *Diary of a Witch*, *The Complete Art of Witchcraft*, and *Moon Signs*. In my eyes, she was a mother of the Craft and a brilliant practitioner. Years after my time at the Magickal Childe, I went to Burley, England, where her store and her flat once stood, and I felt serene as I honored her legend there. There is still such magick there in Burley, and I was struck by the fact that horses are allowed the complete run of the town.

At one point in his life, Herman Slater received a great honor. Raymond Buckland gave Herman his sword to hold and care for. At that time, Raymond was given his own museum (the Buckland Museum of Witchcraft and Magick, in New York). Herman, being a shrewd businessman, took the sword and dismantled it to make molds. There were twenty copies. He gifted the first of these sword copies to Lady Rhea upon her initiation. Eddie Buczynski had one too. Eventually, the original sword was given back to Buckland.

In the 1990s, Lady Rhea had a shop in Yonkers, where she lived with her second husband, Greg (Lord Merlin). They initiated me during a full moon on August 10, 1995. This "elevated" me, as we called it, giving me the Welsh Tradition first. Later on, I earned the Gardnerian Tradition initiations as well, under the umbrella of New York Wica. The Welsh Traditional Gwthoniaid sword was from the Magickal Childe. On an additional note, I had two traditional heirlooms that I have been able to restore. One was a replica of Gardner's sword, which I refurbished and gave to Lady Rhea. The other one is the sword that was given to me from Lord Tammuz, one of the first high priests of the Welsh Traditional Gwthoniaid.

My lineage in the Gardnerian tradition is as follows: Hekatos (me), Lady Rhea, Eddie Buczynski, Lady Sira (Patricia Siero), Theo and Thane (Fran and Gerry Fisher), Lord Robat (Raymond Buckland), Lady Olwen (Monique Wilson), and Gerald Gardner. This is my lineage, despite not being recognized by the hard Gards (nickname for

New York Wica, in the New York Coven of Witches (Photo: Jean Pierre Laffont)

hard-core Gardnerians). Being able to trace my lineage is important because it connects me to Eddie and his legacy. I have deep sympathy for his struggles that gave birth to New York Wica. The Gardnerian Tradition originates from South England. All Gardnerian practitioners copy down Gerald Gardner's book of shadows. Of the three different lines that exist in the United States, I am of the Kentucky line, and thus I am of the lineage of the Silver Trine coven.

Despite my traceable Gardnerian lineage and the fact that I was initiated by a High Priestess and a High Priest, there are those who do not consider me a valid part of the tradition. The objection they have is that Raymond Buckland's wife, Rosemary, was separated from him when he initiated Theo and Thane. You see, it is very important in the Gardnerian Tradition that a High Priest and a High Priestess be present at these initiations. I knew Buckland to be a thorough and elegant man, and it is very unlikely to me that he had no High Priestess at all present, despite these accusations. I am confident that he followed proper protocols when conducting the rite, and I trust the above lineage to be valid. Under any circumstance, my initiatory rite was into a family that honored the old ways wholeheartedly, and that has been good enough for me. I am proud of my lineage.

Returning now to my visits to the Magickal Childe, I remember with joy the interactions I had with Eddie Buczynski. I could not help but to be in total awe of him! He utterly bewitched me with his marvelous green eyes. It filled me with delight when those green eyes eventually came back to visit, and he spiritually guided me to his own traditions, New York Wica and the Welsh.

I admired Eddie Buczynski right away

Edmund Buczynski (January 28, 1947–March 16, 1989). Welsh traditionalist, Gardnerian (New York Wica), and founder of the Minoan Brotherhood.

In my talks with Eddie, I learned that he was a second-degree Welsh traditionalist under Gwen Thompson, a hereditary witch and Celtic traditionalist. Gwen Thompson's given name was Phyllis Healey, and she was from North Haven, Connecticut. She claimed to have hereditary witchcraft, originally from Somerset, England, and then from Nova Scotia to the United States. I was taught that Thompson copied down the text of "The Rede of the Wiccae," a poem believed to have been originally penned hundreds of years ago. She is known for sending the long version of the Wiccan Rede to *Green Egg Magazine*. She founded the New England Coven of Traditionalist Witches in the late 1960s.

Eddie achieved the second degree in the Welsh Tradition while working as a high priest with Lady Gwen, and he took on the craft name of Hermes Dionysus. I have attention deficit disorder (ADD), and since Eddie had a very limited attention span as well, that made him a wonderful teacher for me. I loved how he had a spiritual guru presence, and I really looked up to him. However, he could not fully enjoy his experience, due to the fact that Lady Gwen was so infatuated with him. She made it clear what she desired, but because of Eddie's sexual orientation, nothing could ever happen between them romantically. (After Gwen Thompson, he created his own book of shadows, which is both his legacy and hers.)

Lady Gwen Thompson in a red robe

Later, Eddie appointed Kaye Flagg (Lady Vivienne) as a high priestess of the New York Welsh Tradition. Very early on in life, she found herself captivated by the Goddess. In first grade, Kaye regarded the Marian necklaces (Catholic necklaces the girls were wearing at school) with admiration. Devotion to Mary felt right. However, Kaye had a hard time devoting herself to Jesus, one she saw as dead, lifeless on the crucifix. It was not until the seventh grade that she discovered the Greek and Roman gods and goddesses. Later in life, Kaye moved to New York City, where she met Eddie. They bonded very well, because they both had similar views about the magick of the goddesses and gods. Eddie saw that she was an excellent candidate to become his high priestess. A year and a day before she became initiated into the first, second, and third degrees (in the year 1971), Eddie presented her with his book of shadows to copy down for herself. In addition to being a fabulous high priestess (and a personal friend of mine), Kaye was a brilliant seamstress, singer, and hairdresser. On November 12, 2020, she passed away. I send Lady Vivien blessings to her spirit in the Summerland. She is missed.

In the early 1970s, Eddie went to the Long Island branch, where he learned the Gardnerian Tradition and obtained their first, second, and third degrees. With his third degree, he became a High Priest. He was certainly received as a qualified high priest, but because of his sexual orientation, they discouraged him from acting in the role of Gardnerian High Priest. They thought that he would not be a good role model, or a functional priest, because they wanted the principle of gender (female and male) to remain intact. Even though there were, indeed, principles of polarity at issue, Eddie was really discouraged because they discriminated against him due to his sexuality. Rather than give up, he chose to rise above the discrimination and find his ministry.

To do this, Eddie chose to form a tradition called New York Wica, a Gardnerian offshoot tradition with minor changes. New York Wica allows same-sex initiations, and it is a tradition that has flourished throughout the world and thrives today. It has put down roots in France, Ireland, South America, and beyond! His ministry was important to many after all. (To learn more about Eddie and his magickal journey, please feel free to read Michael Lloyd's book titled *Bull of Heaven: The Mythic Life of Eddie Buczynski and the Rise of the New York Pagan.*) From New York Wica came the Minoan Brotherhood, an all-male homosexual tradition. After that, he assisted Lady Rhea and Lady Miw in the formation of the Minoan Sisterhood, its all-female counterpart.

Eddie is said to have converted to Catholicism near the end of his life, as he was dying of AIDS, while being held in his mother's loving arms. Many know of this, and there is a lot of criticism heaped upon his memory. Faced with his mortality, and in a climate of so many people proclaiming that it was a punishment for his sexual orientation, Eddie had understandable difficulty, mentally and emotionally. Eddie always saw the Goddess represented in statues of Mary. Under pressure from his mother, and in his weakest moments of illness, he consented to receive Catholic last rites. He always honored his own mother as a representation of his Goddess and couldn't refuse her this important homage to her belief system. His memory should not be besmirched by his deep respect for his mother. His last-rites experience does not constitute a conversion, in fact, although it did reflect his upbringing in the Catholic Church. He lived and died a priest of female divinity.

There is a documentary in the making, as of this writing, about the Magickal Childe and those affiliated thereof. The filmmaker is a man named Anderson Slade, of Crowned and Conquering Productions. About a year ago, he was able to gather many video interviews with those affiliated with the Magickal Childe, including Lady Rhea, Lady Vivienne, and myself. Eddie Buczynski's magickal traditions and Simon's *Necronomicon* are mentioned in the film. On November 24, 2020, Slade released the documentary's trailer on YouTube, but as of this writing no official release date for the film has been announced.

In regard to the highly praised Lady Rhea: I initially met her at the Magickal Childe in 1979.

Like Eddie and Herman, Rhea was such an influencer and pioneer of Wicca. Lady Rhea's captivating soul is responsible for having helped open the doors of Welsh Traditional Gwthoniaid and Gardnerian New York Wica for me. In short, Lady Rhea was the one who nurtured my initial understanding of British Traditional Witchcraft.

One extraordinary thing that Herman did was to print a magazine called *Earth Religion News*. I was a young boy when I was first introduced to this publication that even featured sky-clad practitioners. One of these people was Lady Rhea. She was featured in volume 1, issue 4. Lady Rhea's name is not mentioned by her picture on the issue's cover. Instead, the cover had the following wording: Mother Nature Wants You! That was apt, for Lady Rhea has very much been a Mother Goddess figure to me. This issue became a historical memorabilia item for her.

Some people may not know that the image used for the aforementioned magazine cover was one of two. In 1974, the famous Algerian photojournalist Jean-Pierre Laffont, who founded both Gamma USA and Sygma Photo News agency (said to be the largest photo agency in the world), took pictures of the New York Coven of Witches, which featured Lady Rhea, in Brooklyn while Eddie was alive. The pictures were for an editorial spread for the French *ELLE* magazine. Later, one of the pictures was used for Herman Slater's magazine cover. I got a chance to meet Laffont in person, and I was thrilled to be able to purchase original copies of these photographs from him, which he had personally signed. I still treasure these pictures to this day.

Before going any further with more information about Lady Rhea, I have to briefly mention my upbringing beforehand with a Gardnerian high priest, who was of the White Kroft lineage by Elena Ray Bone. Before Rhea, I was taught some about Wicca by this High Priest. Because he was not a High Priestess, obviously, he could not bring me into the tradition fully. Some Gardnerian Witches will not recognize the initiation of a man if the initiation was through another male; it had to be female to male, male to female. I was under his tutelage for a time, and he played a vital role in my development within British Traditional Witchcraft.

At the Magickal Childe, Lady Rhea was motherly, magickal, and bubbly! Her energy was very effective in luring individuals into the shop. When others beheld her, they were enchanted by her beautiful, dark-brown hair and wondrous smile! For me, as a youngster looking up to her, Lady Rhea earned her name, since she properly personified the Greek mother goddess Rhea.

Rhea nurtured many souls. Her motherly side brought forward her world-renowned candle magick. It all started back when Herman left her in charge of accepting a shipment of candles to the Magickal Childe. Unknown to either Herman or Rhea, within that shipment were pullouts (seven-day candles which could be removed easily from the glass). Herman was irate that Rhea accepted the order. He said to her, "What am I to do, Meshugana broad, with these candles?" Rhea responded, "I will take care of it, Herman." Then she took the candles in the back. After that, Rhea took some glitter and some oil, and within minutes she had created the first "enchanted candle." It was a money spell candle. And it was sold for $3! As a keen businessman, Herman was duly impressed. From then on, he insisted that Rhea make more of those candles. Later on, in 1982, Rhea opened her own shop on 9th Street in the East Village, called Enchantments, with Carol Bulzone, who was also known as Lady Miw. Her candles were especially popular, as were her blended oils.

Years later, in 1994, I had a dream where Eddie appeared. His green eyes haunted me, as always. He had passed away in 1989, and I knew that this was a real spirit visit, rather than a mere dream. In the dream, he told me to search for Lady Rhea. Life had shifted to where I had not seen her since the days of her Enchantments shop, in the late 1980s. I did some research and found her living in Yonkers, New York. The reunion was met by both laughter and tears from days gone by and present circumstances, during which I more fully understood that Eddie's message to me had been to follow the path of the Goddess and honor my elders. On an Esbat in August, when the Wort Moon inhabited the sign of Aquarius, I was elevated to third degree and became a High Priest of the Gardnerian Tradition, as well as Eddie Buczynski's own tradition, New York Wica.

At the reopening of Lady Rhea's shop, Magickal Realms, when it was relocated to City Island (a little island off the Bronx) for a time, we managed to see each other regularly, and we made sure that this time we would keep each other closely woven into the fabric of each other's lives for good. I knew this was necessary, especially since Eddie Buczynski had played such an important part, getting me to carry out his wishes for his beloved High Priestess, Lady Rhea!

Despite the journey of life, coupled by hectic work schedules, we often lose contact with important people, but they always seem to return for a purpose, whether it be for love and commitment or some other higher good. Sometime thereafter, I had a revelation of the old days at Enchantments with me honoring our craft elders, such as Herman Slater and Eddie Buczynski. Eventually, this tradition manifested itself again in the form of Lady Rhea's regular "NYC Meet ups."

With so many years of involvement in the Craft, alongside the wisdom shared on behalf of our elders and other pioneers within the occult community, one constant feature in my life has been the spiritually instrumental witch and elder Eddie Buczynski pushing me to keep his work and love alive. He has come to me on numerous occasions and given me important tasks.

I was inactive for a time, just minding my personal practice and focusing on my career, but in 2009, I had a revelation, where I was lost and stranded in the woods with a baby wolf cub. This little wolf, as it turned out, guided me through the woods. The wolf cub metamorphically transformed into an adult wolf. In this form, it gave me the protection and love that I needed. At that time, I knew that I was destined to return to the craft and make my contributions. I needed to let spirit guide me, and to become a parent wolf for others.

Later, I had a vision of myself at Lady Rhea's Enchantments shop. It appeared to be refurbished. I beheld Herman, Eddie, and Lady Rhea there. In the vision, Eddie said to me, "Again, I task you with helping the High Priestess [Lady Rhea]. She will always be in your heart. You need to help her to honor me." Once I returned to my conscious state, the following affirmation came to me from Goddess: "As I honor my elders, I honor myself." (Little did I know that the revelation would soon become a reality when I did a memorial for Buckland and Welsh High Priest Tammuz in New York, honoring my elders and being honored in turn.)

Back in 2006, Lady Rhea published her book *The Enchanted Formulary: Blending Magickal Oils for Love, Prosperity, and Healing* with Citadel Press. When I was reunited with Lady Rhea a few years afterward, I informed her that I was proud of her work. But I also said that she needed to get more work out to the public. She was, and still is, an amazing witch and elder of the craft, with many bountiful gifts of knowledge and wisdom for all to find sustenance from. It was time for her to remind the world of her grandeur and exercise her motherly craft identity. It took many years for her to have another book published. We added updated content (including new sigils, candles, and spells) and heavily edited the existing content, producing a much-finer work than the original version. It was an arduous task, but I also had to work with the previous publisher to get the rights to the material from the first book reverted to the author (a very time-consuming process). Plus, I had to learn about publishing and what that entailed. Eventually, in the year 2016, I published Lady Rhea's *The Enchanted Candle*, which featured a foreword I

I have always had a magician's soul.

wrote. In that same year, in an attempt to help market her second book, I traveled with her to an event in New Orleans, Louisiana. She was one of the festival's guest presenters, and as such, she made sure to bring copies of her newest book (along with all of her famous candle-making supplies). Later, in 2019, after another long and arduous process of adding content and editing, along with publishing rights procurement, I published Lady Rhea's book *The Enchanted Formulary*, which contained another foreword by me, and I supported her prominent image on the book's cover. Every time Lady Rhea has received the praise and recognition she deserves, I have felt great pride, for she is one of my elders and is precious to me.

My chief elder nowadays is my highly esteemed Reverend Mother Laurie Cabot. I am honored and blessed to be a part of her tradition. My journey with Laurie Cabot can be traced back to 2009, the year I chose to reenergize my spiritual journey (because I had finished my surgical boards and received the vision). I did this by asking to be mentored by the Official Witch of Salem, Laurie Cabot.

Alexander ready for Gardnerian practice.

> Born a witch and a witch I'll stay. Powerful Majick lights my way.
>
> —Laurie Cabot

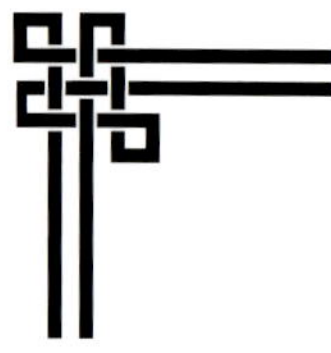
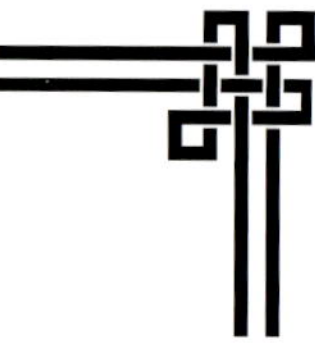

CHAPTER 8
LAURIE CABOT

Before detailing my journey with my Reverend Mother Laurie Cabot, I must first relay my Kemetic heritage, which coincides with Laurie's Cabot's history. At the age of ten, I found myself profoundly captivated by the goddesses and gods of ancient Egypt. They felt timeless, powerful, majickal, and otherworldly. Some of them were shown with wings, and others had animal heads. What I admired most about them was their powerful teachings in Kemeticism, a neopagan majickal tradition that came into the public sphere in the 1970s. Because Kemeticism is a reconstructionist movement, there are many ways in which a Kemetic practitioner may choose to practice. For myself, I found fulfillment in studying the Egyptian Book of the Dead along with *The Kybalion*, by the Three Initiates (Paul Foster Case, a Kemetic initiate, was allegedly the main author of *The Kybalion*; two other initiates associated with that book are said to be William Walker Atkinson and Elias Gewurz, according to *The Kybalion: A Study of the Hermetic Philosophy of Ancient Egypt and Greece*), a book of Hermetic laws that originally are said to have come from the Egyptian god Thoth's emerald tablet. That tablet has been found and studied, according to some sources, and although it is missing a small piece, what can be translated makes up the core basis for alchemy. Here is otherwise the earliest known version (Arabic) of this famous emerald tablet, called the *Pseudo-Apollonius of Tyana's Sirr al-khalīqa wa-san 'at al-tabī'a* (*The Secret of Creation and the Art of Nature*):

حيحص هيف كش ال قح
ىلعألا نم لفسألاو لفسألا نم ىلعألا نإ
دحاو نم اهلك ءايشألا تناك امك دحاو نم بئاجعلا لمع
دحاو ريبدتب
رمقلا همأ ، سمشلا هوبأ
ضرألا هتذغ ،اهنطب يف حيرلا هتلمح
ىوقلا لماك ،بئاجعلا نزاخ ،تامسلطلا وبأ
رانلا نم ضرألا لزعا اضرأ تراص ران
ظيلغلا نم مركأ فيطللا
ىلإ لزنيو ءامسلا ىلإ ضرألا نم دعصي مكحو قفرب
ءامسلا نم ضرألا
لفسألاو ىلعألا ةوق هيفو
ةملظلا هنم برهت كلذلف راونألا رون هعم نأل
ىوقلا ةوق
ظيلغ ءيش لك يف لخدي ،فيطل ءيش لك بلغي
لمعلا نّوكت ربكألا ملاعلا نيوكت ىلع
ةمكحلاب ثّلثملا سمره تيّمس كلذلو يرخف اذهف

English translation (courtesy of David Moore and various translation tools):

Correct, doubtlessly true

Above is from below, and below from above

Work miraculous wonders from one, as all things are of one design

The father is the Sun, the mother is the Moon

The wind carried him in her womb, the earth nursed him

The father of majickal charms, the keeper of wonders and miracles, perfectly full of power

Fire turned into earth, and they separated, the subtle ether from the mundane

Kindness is more present than roughness

Carefully he ascends from earth to heaven, and descends to earth from heaven

He has the power of above and below, because he has the light of lights, so darkness is banished from his presence

This strength energizes and permeates all things, from the etheric to the solid

The whole of creation was formed like this, and upon its structure are all works done

This is my accomplishment, and this is why I am called Hermes Trismegistus, the Triangle of Wisdom, holder of three parts of the wisdom of the universe.

Before I read *The Kybalion*, I had a vision of the Egyptian goddess Isis in statuesque form. She presented herself to me with such grandeur! Isis kneeled to me and spread her wings. She then telepathically directed my eyes to what was the Emerald Tablet of Hermes. The tablet seemed to glow like an actual emerald emitting green light. I understood that this would be important knowledge, and indeed it was, because it would later manifest in the aforementioned Hermetic laws, knowledge, and understanding of the Kemites. From then on, I always had a strong connection to Isis and to Kemetic majick. My spirit knows that the goddess Isis has been with me from the beginning. I intuitively understand and accept that I possess a spiritual lineage to ancient Egypt.

When I beheld the beloved goddess Isis, I was in awe of her winged form. I often imagined her wings and arms around me, protecting me as if I were her son, Horus. My personal vision of Isis holding Horus (me) made me realize the similarity of energy between them and Mother Mary with baby Jesus. When I attended Catholic Mass in my youth, I saw Isis in the faces of the Mary statues.

The Holy Trinity for me was not the Christian Father God, Jesus the Son, and the mysterious Holy Spirit. My holy trinity was that of Osiris (father), Isis (mother), and Horus (son). There was a beauty in this three-person family story, and to me it was cyclical. In order for Horus to be conceived, Isis had to impregnate herself with the manhood of Osiris. After that, Osiris would be reborn, and the process would begin again.

MY FAVORITE PRAYER TO ISIS

Holiest of the holy, perpetual comfort of mankind
You, whose beautiful grace nourishes the entire world
Whose heart turns toward those in sorrow and tribulation
As a mother's to her children
You, ceaselessly offering solace day and night
Always ready to aid the distressed on land and sea
Dispelling gales that beset them
Your hand alone can unravel fate's tangled skeins
End every spell of adverse weather
And prevent harmful celestial conjunctions
The gods above adore you, the gods below pay homage
You set the heavens spinning around the poles
You illuminate the sun, You govern the universe
You subdue the powers of hell
At your command, stars move, seasons return
Earth's spirits rejoice, elements obey
At your signal, winds blow, clouds pour gentle rain
Onto the earth, seeds sprout, buds bloom
Airborne birds, prowling beasts on mountains
Serpents lurking in the dust
All tremble in awe of you.

This prayer was discovered among the remains of a temple of Isis and is exhibited at the Cuming Museum of London History, Walworth Road, Southwark (a borough of London). Remains of an ancient temple dedicated to Isis were actually found in London!

FINDING LAURIE

Laurie Cabot's first teachings were based on Kemetic majick with her coven Black Doves of Isis. In her book *Power of the Witch*, Laurie Cabot writes: "The seven Hermetic Laws are the basis of Witchcraft. Like the laws of physical science, the Hermetic Laws form a system that can be studied by anyone who is willing to put in the effort and take the time to practice" (p. 151).

My first exposure to Laurie Cabot occurred when I was a freshman in high school. It was via the television series *In Search Of*, hosted by Leonard Nimoy. I could not believe that there was a witch, out and proud, in Salem, Massachusetts! Curious to learn more about this spectacular woman, I chose to venture out to Salem with some friends in 1986. While there, I journeyed to Laurie Cabot's shop, Crow Haven Corner, where I met Laurie and her delightful daughter, Penny (who was working behind the register). That establishment was the first witch shop of its kind in the area. It was wonderful for me, a big-city boy who frequented occult shops, to be visiting a small town with a shop completely dedicated to witchcraft.

When I entered the shop, I was at once captivated by the haunting sounds of Kate Bush's "Running Up That Hill." The intoxicating aroma of herbs and the presence of electrifying energy were strongly present in the shop as well. It was in Crow Haven Corner that I purchased my first pentacle. On the way out of the store, I noticed that there was a black Mercedes convertible parked outside. What made me notice this car was the fact that there was a black cat that remained on top of it. Curious, I walked closer to the car to inspect the cat more closely. Surely, this was a stuffed animal? How could a cat choose to remain on the vehicle if it was real? To my bewilderment, the cat's ears went up and its eyes grew wider as I approached. It truly was a real

The Reverend Mother recognizes my efforts, October 2015

cat! (Later I learned that this black cat was Laurie Cabot's familiar, who was tasked with guarding her Mercedes. It certainly did its job.)

On the journey home, I pondered what had occurred in Salem. I grabbed hold of the pentacle I wore around my neck. As I did so, I remembered the power and mystique of Laurie Cabot and her familiar. Little did I know that I would one day journey back to her there and become one of her disciples, and eventually also a High Priest of the Cabot Tradition.

In the 1990s, my spiritual path took me through Spiritualism, Santeria, the New York Welsh Tradition, and Gardnerian–New York Wica, but my spirit longed for more. I had a passionate desire to become a good role model of the Old Religion one day. Years later, this heart's desire gave way for me to reenergize my path by honoring my Celtic heritage via Laurie Cabot's majickal tradition (my specific Celtic heritage comes from Spain, where my ancestors lived in Galicia).

In the year 2008, I was ready to visit Laurie Cabot again. Then I headed to her newest shop, The Cat, The Crow, and The Crown. It was very much like its predecessor in atmosphere; it was beautiful and majickally alluring. The visit spoke to me again on a deep level, but it was just a visit. However, a year later, I visited Laurie again in the same store and got up the nerve to approach her. I informed her that I felt my Goddess had called me to start my path with her in order to honor my Celtic heritage (what better person than Laurie Cabot for that?). I recall that she admitted that she vaguely remembered me. However, she could see that I was sincere in my desire to become her student. She kindly gifted me a dram of money oil, a money-drawing potion that I still have to this day. I beamed with excitement at the accepting gesture, and I thanked her for her thoughtful gift. After that, I told her that I still had an original postcard that I bought from her shop in the 1980s that she had signed for me. Frankly, I was giddy and a little starstruck.

Not long after this encounter, I began my training as a Cabot witch. Almost every time there was a new training session, I traveled by bus for four hours each way, from New York City to Salem. It was very important to me that I did my best to make it to these many classes in person (I took just very few of them online). Through my dogged perseverance, I managed to achieve the first, second, and third degrees of the Cabot Tradition.

The first degree pertains to the first principle of Hermeticism, which is mentalism and exercising psychic gifts. The second degree teaches witchcraft and the related tools. The third degree lasted a year and a day, an important concept in time coming from the Celtic lore that ancient Celts did not recognize one day of the year, so one had to add a day of training in order to complete a full year of training, a full sun cycle in its entirety. For me, this training process was like going back to public school all over again. I had school every weekend, with books I had to read. I also had to attend classes every month. After the third-degree studies, with the many struggles and long trips it took to complete the year and a day, I had to go through clergy classes, which lasted another six to eight months. These clergy classes were arduous but thorough. The practitioner would become a bona fide clergyman, equipped with the skill to perform and adapt all needed rites, while being a civil servant minister. The classes gave me the ideology and theology and mythology; plus, I got to service the public. I was taught how to conduct myself in public. I was taught how to troubleshoot problems and go through trials and tribulations with others. The clergy classes were an adjunct to her teaching that made me feel more prepared and fulfilled in her ministry. This was a test for me of devotion and perseverance, for me to know what I truly wanted. Finally, wanting to prove my utmost desire to be a part of her tradition and to help it grow, I petitioned to be initiated and ordained as a High Priest. My petition was granted, and I was also later given the great honor of becoming the Cabot Tradition ambassador to Brazil!

BRAZIL

In 2014, several groups were asking for representation from great pioneers of witchcraft in America. One, in particular, was Wicca do Brasil (Brazil). This group had an event every autumn equinox where participants would march within an ecumenical parade. (Laurie Cabot chose the word "ecumenical" because it is a Latin word, meaning "the coming of churches.") The word "ecumenical" encompasses the event because the event involves many Christian denominations walking together through the streets of Copacabana in Rio de Janeiro. In addition to the plethora of Christian denominations, the parade had polytheistic faiths represented as well. There were Buddhists, Spiritists (especially the devotees of Allan Kardec), and those of the Afro-Brazilian diaspora. They wanted the Cabot Tradition represented in it!

As it so happened, I was asked to be a representative of the Cabot Tradition following my ordination (I was invited to come to Brazil, with some expenses paid). Laurie Cabot and Penny Cabot encouraged me to accept this offer, because they knew of my earlier involvement with Brazil, due to my medical career. This connection was created through an aesthetic surgical conference I attended with my surgeon, Ivo Pitanguy, one of the most renowned plastic surgeons in the world, who had lived in Brazil. I was tasked with assisting in live surgery from Santos, Brazil, and then to São Paulo. This visit was my first experience in Brazil. This all occurred in the year 2003. I made great friends in Brazil. I met a wonderful Brazilian family who had Castilian roots and had achieved a measure of financial success in Brazil. They had two lovely children, who grew up and became my friends. I love them to pieces! They are a cherished part of my Brazilian family.

Becoming the Cabot ambassador to Brazil was my first mission as an ordained minister. My mission was to teach people about Laurie Cabot's body of work, her tradition, and the temple. The event in Brazil was run

Taken in Brazil while representing the Cabot Tradition

by various groups, but it was done cooperatively for the purpose of promoting religious tolerance. Prior to the procession, I was invited to speak at a university in Rio de Janeiro. Now that I think back on this, I remember that I spoke for two hours and gave my presentation in a filled auditorium. They were awarding college credits to students for attending the Wicca presentation. There were many guest speakers, but I was the only foreign guest speaker. After the symposium, there was the aforementioned parade for religious tolerance. I was also featured on Brazilian television, speaking on religious tolerance while representing the Cabot Tradition. I spoke what is called Portuñol (a combination of Portuguese and Spanish, similar to Spanglish = Spanish/English) and was understood well enough.

WHAT IT MEANS TO BE A CABOT

During my training to become a high priest, I took the name Cabot. The name was a convenient way for me to separate my identity as a witch from my also somewhat public professional life. Taking the name also helped me honor Laurie Cabot's legacy wherever I go. I became publicly known as Alexander Cabot. This has been a great honor that I have cherished. You see, upon earning the third degree, many Cabot witches have taken on the name as a public middle name, but only a few have been given the right to use the name as a surname or pen name as I was, following in Laurie's footsteps.

The Cabot Tradition has a code of ethics. Every Cabot witch has to abide by the code in order to remain in good standing with the tradition. Here is a list of these ethics, written by Reverend High Priest James Daily for the Cabot Tradition:

CABOT CODE OF ETHICS

ONE: We abide by the Threefold Law of Return and "An it harm none, do what ye will."

TWO: Treat others in our tradition as you would like to be treated. We are Witch sisters and brothers.

THREE: We recognize a Cabot Witch of any degree as a part of our tradition.

FOUR: Integrity, Discipline, and Respect must be self-evident in all our affairs as we represent our Tradition.

FIVE: We practice our craft according to Hermetic Laws, and we are accountable to the God/Goddess/ALL.

SIX: We do not accept any outside contributions or influences that would undermine our authority. We are a sovereign tradition. As such, we do not take part in the inner circles of other traditions.

SEVEN: Each Cabot Witch is Sovereign and accepts the Responsibility that this incurs.

EIGHT: We are committed to our way of life and firmly grounded in the Science of our majick. We express our Tradition as an Art, a Science, and a Religion.

NINE: We respect and adhere to the wishes of our Council of Elders.

TEN: Our Tradition has an interest in issues such as ecology, hunger, and human rights. We seek to heal and protect our Mother Earth and better the lives of the humans and animals around us through majickal and charitable means.

ELEVEN: Our public relations policy is based on attraction rather than promotion; we do not proselytize. We do try to educate anyone that seeks knowledge from us.

TWELVE: We place principles before personalities. We abstain from gossip and other behaviors that would undermine our brothers and sisters or our Tradition. Our actions reinforce "for the good of all."

THIRTEEN: We do not charge money for taking healing cases but may charge for any type of psychic consulting to the public as a reader (e.g., Tarot).

"Sovereign" refers to our individual power, used for the good of others. We are taught to take responsibility for how we use our abilities gained. Sovereignty is not just for a person to use to rule over others for personal gain; for us it means to use all of our might to properly serve others and to provide an upstanding example. "Majick" is a spelling used within the Cabot Tradition, to set our ways apart. Ultimately, we understand that the goal of majick is to transmute our soul (mind, will, and emotions) along with our spiritual knowledge and understanding into higher vibrations.

LAURIE CABOT'S DEGREES: DOING THE WORK

I did so much traveling for the classes and never regretted a moment of it. I distinctly remember that the journey and commitment of traveling from New York City to Salem, Massachusetts, during the month of March aligned with the Sun sign of Pisces one day, and that marked an exceptional occasion, since Laurie Cabot would be teaching on her eightieth birthday. I arranged for the creation and delivery of a unique, lifelike doll of her by a renowned doll maker in São Paulo, Brazil. This gift aimed to be the centerpiece of a special moment during the reunion, teachings, and birthday festivities. With the help of Penny, her daughter, we organized a small celebration at her workshop in the legendary "The Cat, Crow & Crown Shoppe," later known as "The Official Witch Shoppe" in its final iteration. Perched on the Pickering Wharf, overlooking the Atlantic Ocean, the shop's atmosphere and breezy energy were invigorating. That week coincided with the moon's zenith, aligning multiple cosmic variables. The CCC ranch, as some called it, served as the epicenter for Laurie's merchandise, teachings, meditations, and communal gatherings.

Subsequently, I pursued the second degree, which emphasized herb craft, spellcraft, ritual, astrology, and utilizing nature's tools. This continued at the same location, rekindling the mentorship within her environment. The third degree unexpectedly followed, contrary to the customary waiting period of a year and a day before undertaking this significant step within her tradition. She sensed our readiness this time and bypassed the waiting period, inviting us into her most cherished degree, solidifying our commitment to the craft. This memorable event occurred at her home on Pickering Wharf, marking a profound time spent with her, which I really cherish to this day. As she transitioned her merchandise online and began teaching virtually, the physical shop was dismantled.

Being instructed by her was a loving experience steeped in majick. I recognized that perseverance and dedication would serve as my anchors on the path to becoming part of her priesthood and the realm of the goddess. My journey had unique facets, extending beyond the third degree to encompass clergy classes held at an elder's home every Friday for six months. This comprehensive course prepared us for our priesthood and service to the Goddess.

To finalize my initiation and ordination, I engaged in a profound conversation with Laurie and Penny,

I had a doll custom-made in Brazil for the Reverend Mother's eightieth birthday.

expressing my true intentions for the clergy. I articulated that my inspiration stemmed from my Celtic heritage and a New York City elder, Margot Adler, whom I had known and met years ago. This calling originated from the Goddess.

One of my revelations concerning divinity involves the transformative state of mind. Through years of meditation—a crucial exercise for spiritual growth—I experienced an epiphany characterized by vibrational fluidity intertwined with emotions. This revelation illuminated the key for any spell or prayer: the essential role of emotions alongside intent and devotion. Our emotions, coupled with meditative practices, generate a powerful vibrational frequency required to reach divinity. In essence, our EMOTIONS serve as the primary force linking us to polarity, and balance embodies divinity. Much like Buddha's quest for divinity, exposing emotions, intellect, and oneself to the spectrum of polarities reveals divinity within balance.

I've often realized the pivotal role that emotions play in tapping into divinity. Affirmations, manifestation, prayers, chanting mantras, and incantation and spell casting all fall under the umbrella of intent and self-development. They serve as tools for the mind, and soul and are diverse exercises. Chanting mantras, originating from ancient cultural philosophies, taps into self-vibrational frequencies through repetitive use in meditative practices, aiding the mind in achieving its objectives.

Affirmations bolster self-esteem, empowerment, and other life goals, providing inner strength. Prayer and manifestation, age-old practices, encompass spirituality in all religions, addressing emotional needs and gratitude. Incantations, through verbalization, and spell casting, through action, have ancient origins in various cultures and folklore. They operate through the trajectory of emotions, harnessing the highest and purest frequencies of the physical and spiritual realms.

WITCHCRAFT INITIATIONS

There are many conflicting thoughts on the importance of initiations in witchcraft. Initiatory witchcraft is extremely important to me, so I want to share some thoughts on the subject while I'm thinking about them in my Cabot Tradition background. There are various spiritual paths one can choose or that may simply be destined for one to stumble upon, depending on our understanding and perception of will and fate. I firmly believe that communal energies are catalytic for our spiritual growth and intellectual development, and also for learning to act with wisdom. Our inner spiritual drive motivates us to reach and fill the void most of us become aware of at some point in our development, our spiritual need. Regardless of the traditions we engage with, I always assert that "we never stop learning; even at ninety, we are still learning from the young, the old, and nature itself."

Initiation has several important facets to consider: It's a new beginning, a milestone on our spiritual journey, an accomplishment, the overcoming of an obstacle, an introduction for those proven qualified for a new level of development. It's all of those things and more to me, but especially I feel, deep in my heart, that it signifies acceptance from my chosen spiritual family, and it is accompanied by a sense of belonging that I think isn't peculiar to me. It's a natural human need to feel accepted, and to understand our place in our human family. All of my personal initiation experiences, across the many varied traditions, have been profoundly special to me. As an only child and often a loner in my daily life, I cannot express in print how deeply I appreciate what initiations have brought to my quality of life.

Beyond these aspects of initiation, in my understanding it is a test as well, requires commitment from the initiate, and is a beckoning of one's individual spirituality to a new level of development. It often involves intense emotions, deep contemplation, and perseverance. It stands as a rite of passage leading to another significant stage of growth and subsequent adventure ahead. Initiation means start, and it is definitely a new start every time. We never stop learning and growing, as I mentioned.

We live in a polarized world, full of divisions and weighted sides of issues. Balance is a key part of rites of passage. I've encountered obstacles and obstructions from multiple sources along the way, contributing to building the strength and understanding to counter these forces. I feel that my initiations and the training leading to and from them have equipped me to do so.

Shown on p. 114 is me holding a special gift quartz crystal, given at my third-degreee initiation at the Cabot Kent Hermetic Temple. It really meant the world to me at that moment. Some facts that people may know about quartz are that it is the most common of all minerals, it comes in many forms, and it varies in size from tiny particles glittering on the surface of a rock to pieces that weigh up to a ton. It can be transparent or translucent. In its natural state, it is colorless, but frequently it is colored by impurities. Some common resulting colors of quartz are rose, smoky, amethyst, and green. These types of the crystal may be used in jewelry and in decorative pieces. For witches, though, quartz crystals are used not for their looks, but because of their vibrations and natural qualities, to help us with psychic skills and attunement of them, to stabilize our energy flow, and for directing or storing energy.

Holding my third-degree-initiation gift, a large quartz crystal *(Photo: Richard Santana)*

In my practice, crystals have always helped me channel and focus my natural psychic abilities, stabilize my personal energies, and stimulate my creativity and vision. I heard crystals calling to me, even as a child, and I felt the energy vibrating through me, and I listened to their frequencies. Much later, I learned of the use of quartz in timepieces. I was amazed when I realized that there was scientific basis for the frequencies that I was hearing, that people have measured those frequencies and documented them and then felt joy, that my experiences seemed so much more valid. It really feels great to be part of a tradition that combines science with majick in such meaningful ways.

THE REVEREND MOTHER

Laurie Cabot is a trailblazer! She is a pioneer who has dedicated herself to the preservation of the old gods and the Craft. Her majickal tradition is composed of three things: art, science, and religion. Part of learning to practice witchcraft is becoming able to exercise creativity to ensure that one's personal energy is infused in the workings. We are invested in our work. Witchcraft is a scientific discipline because witchcraft is based on the Hermetic laws, which correspond to quantum physics and quantum mechanics and formed the basis of early chemistry.

THE BLUE LIGHT OF JUPITER

During the filming and photography for an editorial spread by *National Geographic* on the New England shore area, they visited Salem, a historically significant seaport in America. The name "Salem" shares its origins and meaning with the word "shalom," a Hebrew greeting of peace. In fact, this word for peace is a word rendered as "salom" in various other Semitic languages like Arabic. This background set the stage for Salem to evolve into an inclusive and diverse village.

Laurie Cabot's original coven, the Black Doves of Isis, held their summer solstice ritual during this visit by *National Geographic*, and they did a working to summon the blue light of Jupiter for prosperity. The photographers documented the event, taking photographs when they were allowed to. When the film was developed, the team discovered, much to their shock, a blue lightning-like phenomenon surrounding the coven in every exposure. Fascinated, they visited Laurie multiple times seeking explanations, until she demanded to witness the evidence herself. Seeing this phenomenon captured on film delighted her, confirming the result of that ritual. The blue ray of light emanated from the chalice and out onto every member of the coven in the photos. Initially hesitant to publish these images, due to the fear of the unknown, the team debated and delayed, until the administrative director insisted on the photos' publication. Upon release in 1981, it became the most discussed paranormal phenomenon, trending in discussions for quite some time.

A blue lightning-like phenomenon captured in this photo taken during a summer solstice ritual with Laurie Cabot's original coven.

LAURIE CABOT'S TEACHINGS SPOKE TO ME

She was even invited to speak at Salem University about how traditional witchcraft corresponds to modern science. I loved the way Laurie always taught us that witchcraft and science were one and the same, and I have always loved her unique methods of practice. Finally, Cabot practitioners work their spells via the energies of the ancient ones / our ancestors / the mighty ones, some of whom are revered (not worshiped) as goddesses and gods. I personally choose to worship only Source, the All, while I am reverent toward all lesser spirits, which I see as integral parts of the All. I'm essentially a pantheist in practice.

A thing I really appreciate about the Cabot Tradition of cooperating with scientific teachings is Laurie's impressive psychological method, taught in the first-degree classes, to help the practitioner achieve the alpha brain wave state. With this method, devotees are able to train their minds to enter a higher state of awareness. The brain usually works with beta, theta, and delta brain waves, but it is not common practice for humans to enter into the alpha wavelength. It is, however, an ideal state in which to accomplish majick and to develop and use psychic faculties.

Meditation is one of the vital exercises to neutralize chaotic forces and seek balance. For me, it's about tapping into the primordial source of spirit, soul, and consciousness. I stress consciousness because, as I perceive it, awareness resides within the soul, encapsulating history, emotions, and information—the fundamental building blocks of collective consciousness. Dreams, while often venting the subconscious, also serve as a conduit through which we tune into that frequency, establishing a connection with the spirit. Dreams, therefore, present another avenue for organic and spiritual balance. Dreams have played a significant role in harmonizing my daily life, occasionally serving as channels through which I've received crucial information. I've found maintaining a dream journal incredibly useful, since every dream has its interpretation, although we might not grasp it immediately, and their memory often fades. Sometimes, dreams don't offer new information but provide some form of confirmation. During my surgical career, several times I've encountered ENT (ear, nose, and throat) surgeons whose practices include sleep studies—an undeniably fascinating subject. I love learning from them, and I know that a restful night's sleep has often enriched my perspective on life.

THE STAGES OF BRAIN WAVES

Gamma (>30 Hz)
Beta (13–30 Hz)
Alpha (8–12 Hz)
Theta (4–8 Hz)
Delta (<4 Hz)

During my childhood, I was taught to perceive the alpha brain wave state as semiconsciousness, which we understood as the ultimate meditative state. Incorporating this into our daily routine can be a beneficial exercise. Having a specific mantra, affirmation, or prayer that aids in reaching this heightened consciousness is ideal.

LAURIE CABOT'S BRILLIANT METHOD FOR ACHIEVING ALPHA STATE

First, the witch closes his or her eyes and pictures a black screen. Then they see the number 7 in red, 6 in orange, 5 in yellow, 4 in green, 3 in blue, 2 in indigo, and 1 in orchid. From red 7 down to orchid 1, they cascade slowly before the mind's eye. For us, this method is called the Crystal Countdown, and it is based on proven psychological methodology. It is extraordinary how well this technique works to prepare oneself for majickal workings, and it's also very easy to learn. This method is a staple for all of us in the Cabot Tradition, and I have never seen it anywhere else before. Sure, when studying with mediums, I had been taught to enter a meditative state with a sort of similar blank screens, but it took much longer to learn it. This method was making efficient practitioners out of fairly new people in a relatively short time. Impressive indeed!

MORE ON THE CABOT TRADITION

The Cabot Tradition of witchcraft has a physical brick-and-mortar location called the Cabot Kent Hermetic Temple. It was created as a 501(c)(3), an officially recognized federal nonprofit organization and legal church. The temple became the first federally recognized temple of witchcraft in the history of Salem, Massachusetts. Its mission is to educate the masses about witchcraft, as it correlates with modern science, and to help serve the community.

The Crystal Wheel, invented by Laurie Cabot, was first practiced by the aforementioned Black Doves of Isis coven in the late 1970s. Essentially, the Crystal Wheel was a construct on the astral plane that hovers above Salem high in the sky, a work manifested by many years of creative meditation work of many Cabot witches in Salem, Massachusetts. Today, it is seen as a huge wheel, completely composed of crystal, that one can tap into with the mind in meditation, viewing with the third eye, in order to focus the energies of healing for those in need, including ourselves. It is a conduit, a medium through which our work may cooperate and be concentrated and magnified. In my mind's eye, it has always looked like a huge wheel-shaped and glistening satellite in our atmosphere, collecting and directing energies. Every Thursday night at 10:00 EST (North American Eastern Standard Time, as in New York), unified energies of all Cabot witches (and others) join power with the Crystal Wheel.

Another technique that is singular to the Cabot Tradition is the use of a gaming board. Here is an excerpt from Laurie Cabot's recently published *Book of Shadows* regarding the board:

> The gaming board is a tool no other tradition uses. While today we relate it to the game of chess, our ancestors related it to the Game of Life. In the Celtic traditions, it was known as Fidchell in Irish, and was said to be the invention of the god Lugh. In the Welsh traditions, it was known as Gwyddbwyll, and it shows up in the myth known as The Dream of Rhonabwy, a tale of King Arthur. The gaming board consists of sixty-four black and white squares. We use it as the centerpiece for our altar and set symbols upon it. You can use it for both spellcraft and divination, though some keep two separate gaming boards for those purposes. We place chess pieces, symbols, roots, talismans, and stones upon it when casting spells. In the center of the board, you place a symbol of yourself. Bring things to you from the left, using black squares to help you manifest things. Send things out or away to the right and place them upon white squares. You can speed majick by moving things around your board.

It is not part of my regular practice to make use of the Cabot Gaming Board. However, what I do use is an altar (credenza) made of oak, fashioned for me by a wonderful Argentinian friend. Before I became a Cabot witch, my altar already had a chessboard on it. I chose to have my credenza feature the chessboard because of my Freemasonry heritage (Masonic Lodge floors are black and white tiles, as were the floors of Solomon's temple, according to legend), along with the polarity of the yin and yang. My Kemetic background also comes into play with my love of the gaming board: as above, so below. According to the Kybalion, "Everything is Dual; everything has poles; everything has its pair of opposites; like and unlike are the same; opposites are identical in nature, but different in degree; extremes meet; all truths are but half-truths; all paradoxes may be reconciled." It felt natural to me, then, that the Cabot gaming board would be used as a spell-casting tool later in my life.

OUR WHEEL OF THE YEAR

Each year has two sides to it: the light and dark periods. These parts are divided into eight parts in the witch's year. This set of eight parts represents the eight Sabbats. They are known as the historical, cultural, and agricultural Wheel of the Year. To be precise, many tribes would celebrate only four occasions, the two solstices and two equinoxes, as the high holy Sabbats. Witches adopted the other four Sabbats on the basis of historical findings, as part of the amalgamated creations of neopagan traditions, reclaiming and reconstructing our ancestral ways.

The first one of the eight Sabbats marks the beginning of the witch's year. It is known as Samhain. It is celebrated on October 31 (the same date as Halloween, and by no accident, for it is the original observance that eventually became Halloween). Usually, the Reverend Mother designs and writes a fresh ritual for the occasion each year. It is her high holy holiday, and she personally takes charge of the festivities and observances.

I remember a time, back in the 1980s, when Salem, Massachusetts, was less inhabited than it is now. Halloween was quaint, even charming. Haunted happenings were at their beginnings there. Salem once had an Old-World charm. Over the years, many nicknames have been given to Salem—Halloween Center, Witch City, and others. It's best to visit Salem at this time of year if you are a novice or tourist. In recent years, Salem has become a popular tourist spot, and people love having their picture taken with the statue of Elizabeth Montgomery (from the popular TV show *Bewitched*). I usually choose to travel to Salem at less congested times, since I'm not fond of such large crowds. Let's examine the other seven Sabbats, in a Cabot family traditional sense.

Yule (winter solstice, around December 21): At Yule, we make our own ornaments to decorate the Yule tree, representing the large Cabot family. We take the time to honor our Reverend Mother's many years of teaching, and we generally give her gifts. We usually take part in Toys for Tots and other ways of giving to less fortunate children and families. One significant thing we always do in our ritual is the "changing of the guard," wherein we enact the battle between the Holly King and the Oak King, after which the winner, the Oak King, begins his reign as the sun is reborn. Traditionally, our dear Ernest has played the role of the Holly King, and we love him for it. Our beloved Reverend Memie Watson always delights us with her representation of the sugarplum fairy.

Imbolc (February 1): Our Celtic heritage really shines at Imbolc, where we focus our adoration on the Goddess Bridgit. Goddess Brigid, pronounced like "breed" in the Welsh, and sometimes presented as Brid, Brighid, Bride, Brigit, and Brigitte, depending on the language, always was the Celtic goddess I have gravitated toward. As a young boy, I especially enjoyed Imbolc. My family would hold the door ajar and light the votive candle for goddess Brigid to enter. Her warm hearth flame was my inspiration. I always liked Lugh, who was a radiant and captivating avatar of god to me as well, as the god of the golden light of the sun. Here is an inspired invocation to Brigid:

INVOCATION TO BRIGID, BY ALEXANDER CABOT

Goddess of reddish-golden hair,
With the door ajar on the Eve of Imbolc,
May you light as a Candle is lit in your name.

Ostara (spring or vernal equinox, March 21): The first thing I personally think of is the connection with the white hare and Ostara. She was said to have turned a bird into a hare, and the hare then laid colored eggs that were used in her festival. She carries the symbol of newborn life, fertility, nature awakening. Because she has a fairy ministry, Reverend High Priestess Jacq Civitarese is usually responsible for presiding over this Sabbat.

Beltane (May Day, May 1): Cabots celebrate this lovely holiday by allowing the children to adorn the mayPole in the temple, guided by High Priests and High Priestesses to weave the ribbons. The children really love this activity, and we like to keep the focus on them. We honor the horned god Cernunnos, and we regard this as the first of the fire-related rites of the year, marking the sacred spark of life that bore all other life. Our Canadian chapter—namely, Lady Leslie and Lord Jeff—is always honored with the responsibility for designing and writing the ritual for Beltane each year in collaboration with the Reverend High Priestess Bree Bella Cabot as of this writing.

Litha (summer solstice, June 21–22): I have always really enjoyed celebrating the summer solstice. Litha, Gathering Day, and Midsummer are a few of its names. Cabots love creating decorations together to honor our God and Goddess at Litha, and various High Priests and Priestesses are given the honor of writing the ritual and presiding over the festivities. We always enact the battle of the Oak King and the Holly King again, and the victor this time is the Holly King, as the sun wanes and the nights begin to take the advantage over the days.

Lammas (Lughnassad, August 1): Cabots venerate Lugh at this time, and I once wrote this invocation to him: "Lugh, god of strength, with your mighty spear, come forth and bring your glow upon us as I anoint the golden candle." This occasion has long marked the first major harvest of the year, and we often decorate with wheat.

Mabon (autumnal equinox, September 21): We reenact the mother, Modron, weeping for her child, Mabon, from the Mabinogion. I recall that we decorated with a lot of autumn leaves, all of the orange, brown, and red. We hold this occasion to be the witches' Thanksgiving, and we do a communal Thanksgiving dinner.

THE LEGEND LIVES ON

As she has recently reached her ninety-second birthday, as of this edition, the Reverend mother still teaches. She honors us all with her presence on social media. Laurie Cabot was exceptional when she agreed to perform readings for the masses during the 2020 pandemic. She is an icon and a force to be reckoned with in Salem, Massachusetts, and beyond. Cabot extends her legacy

Illustration by Wiccarts

to her clergymen, which I carry on with dignity, integrity, and respect. I will always be grateful to her for her many contributions to the craft and to my own life.

Penny was asked about her impressions and memories of me. Penny recounts, "I first recall meeting Alexander in the Faerie Grotto of Laurie Cabot's old shop, standing under the indoor Hawthorn faerie tree. Over his head was a hand-painted banner sign, welcoming the Tuatha de Dannan to the place. Behind him, poems of Yeats decoupaged the walls on parchment paper, with the words stained brown with tea. Alexander was signing up for class. This was the beginning of a new spiritual journey for him in the Cabot Tradition. I saw an elegant man with a face full of adventure, starting a path that would prompt him to weigh and question everything. Majick, when you ask it, will pull from the universal mind specially designed tasks (ego vs. kindness, self-love vs. self-worth, and so on), helping the querant to grow. His new journey had begun. At the time, I didn't know how much he had already experienced. It turned out that this was just a new chapter of the book of shadows his life wrote. From Danu to Cerridwen, Alexander learned and grew, moving through the carefully prepared path. He was warmly cared for in this well-stocked community, lit with kindness and the love of self and home. He was always protected by his majick, consistent and intentional. Here we are, more than a decade later, and I find myself writing to you about Alexander Cabot, Reverend High Priest of the Cabot Tradition and ambassador to Brazil. Alexander has found his personal sovereignty through the knowledge and tradition he gained. He honors the gods and goddesses, especially the great mother, with gratitude and humility. I am very proud to present the words of his life and lessons, and proud to call him my Cabot brother."

The Green Minister
Cabot Kent Hermetic Temple
Reverend Penny Cabot, High Priestess

This original painting is by Penny Cabot, depicting Hekate. Among many other things, I associate Hekate with the bee, since it was said that Medea, niece of the great witch Circe, and a priestess of Hekate, used hypnotized bees in her summoning of Hekate. Herodotus called Medea the Great Goddess of the Aryan tribes of

Penny Cabot, Hekate

Parthia, and Pliny the Elder wrote that her majick controlled the sun, moon, and stars. What a powerful symbol of Hekate, then, bees are!

A friend of mine whom I knew from my days at the Magickal Childe gave me the lyrics to a song, which I have always seen as a spell to invoke Hekate:

A SLEEPIN' BEE

It was originally written for the 1954 musical *House of Flowers*, based on the Truman Capote novella by the same name. Set in Haiti, the production featured a trio of steel drummers (known as pannists) from Trinidad. It was composed by Harold Arlen, and the lyrics were written by Truman Capote and Harold Arlen in 1954 (one of the versions is shown here, as sung by Barbra Streisand—see also the Tony Bennett version for another perspective):

When a bee lies sleepin'
In the palm of your hand
You're bewitched, and deep in
Love's long-looked-after land
Where you'll see a sun-up sky
With a mornin' moon
And where the days go laughin'
By, as love comes a callin' on you
Sleep on bee, don't waken
Can't believe what just passed
He's mine for the takin'
I am happy at last
Maybe I dreams
But he seems
Sweet golden as a crown
A sleepin' bee
Done told me
I will walk with my feet off the ground
When my one true love, I has found
Sleep on bee, don't waken!
Cannot believe what just passed!
He's mine for the takin'
I am happy at last
Maybe I dreams
But he seems
Golden as a crown
A sleepin' bee
Told me
I will walk with my feet off the ground
When my one true love, I has found!

In honor of my Reverend Mother and to illustrate my deep appreciation for the Cabot Tradition, I leave the reader with the following incantation that I wrote:

As I use Jupiter oil from Laurie Cabot,
I anoint the Goddess and the God candle.
I go into Alpha.
I bring forth masculine and feminine.
As I light this candle,
From Goddess, wisdom is born
Unto Male Divinity, knowledge is given.
So shall it be.

We swear by peace and love to stand
Heart to heart, and hand in hand
Mark, O Spirit, and hear us now
Confirming this, our sacred vow.
—Druid Oath of Peace

I have had the honor and privilege to meet with Alexander on two separate occasions, at the Managed Open Access at Stonehenge, and I have found him to be knowledgeable and capable as a Reverend High Priest, possessing the twin qualities of quiet reverence and charisma in equal measure, a rare balance indeed in the Pagan community. I am happy to call him my friend and fellow traveler on this journey.

—King Arthur Pendragon

Senior Druid and Pagan Priest

Arthur Pendragon and I at Stonehenge

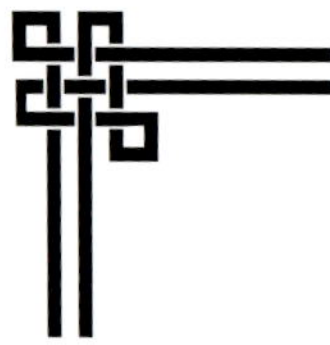

CHAPTER 9

CELESTIAL STONES

On a few special occasions, I have visited England, and I certainly plan to go again. It has been a major highlight each time to visit Stonehenge, a prehistoric formation of stones found in the countryside of Wiltshire. The stones average 13 feet high and 7 feet wide. Each stone weighs approximately 25 tons. Stonehenge is one of the most recognized structures in the world, and it is one that I have always felt spiritually linked to.

It wasn't always as we see it today. There are artists' representations and archeologists' approximations of what it once looked like, but the ruins were in a less preserved state in 1901 than they appear to be today. In that year, at least one stone was straightened and set in concrete, to prevent it from falling and harming someone. More-detailed renovations were carried out in the 1920s, when at least six stones were erected and fortified, and again later there were more restoration actions taken. Most of the stones that stand now were fallen over the ages, and were raised again at the turn of the century, according to some sources. An article by Emma Young in 2001, found online at NewScientist.com, says, "Most of the one million visitors who visit Stonehenge on Salisbury Plain every year believe they are looking at untouched 4,000-year-old remains. But virtually every stone was re-erected, straightened, or embedded in concrete between 1901 and 1964," and she credits a British doctoral student. It isn't just Stonehenge—many of the stones at Avebury were erected in the 1930s. Whether what we see is the true original location and formation of the stones or not, I maintain that there is a tangible spiritual quality about the place and those stones, and they call me back to them.

The first time I visited Stonehenge was with a tour group, moving through many of the megalithic structures and other ancient wonders of England. I had a big birthday coming, and I wanted to celebrate with the natural energies and ancient greatness of the United Kingdom. I had my Cabot sister, Tracy Claudio, with me on this trip. It was the autumn of 2015 when we traveled there, and for the autumnal equinox we were introduced by an acquaintance to a group of Druids and allowed to be present for the "Rising of the Sun" ceremony led by Arthur Pendragon and held at the famous Stonehenge site! As we approached the campgrounds at four in the morning, we were stopped by guards from English Heritage, an official organization that cares for over four hundred historic monuments throughout England. We were told to head to another section of the campgrounds that was reserved for the Druids and observers (we were observers, of course). We then waited until the procession began. As we entered the path, led by the druidic order, I felt like I was stepping in the footsteps of our ancestors to this Neolithic structure.

What was it originally created for? Was it used for something else at other times in its long history? There have been so many hypotheses about the original purpose or repurposing of the Stonehenge site, from it once being a temple to it being a burial ground, from an astronomical observation site to a method of plotting courses to navigate the oceans. Some saw it as a place of sacrifice, others a place of lost ancient technology and evidence of ancient scientific disciplines. Some point out that it is built upon a large intersection of ley lines, and others point to its location on global coordinates and alignments with other ancient sites. Some point to aliens, others to gods, and still others to lost ancient human technology. A few have proven that it can be built by humans with only the most-basic materials, and others insist that it would have been impossible for people back then to create. I've looked at the debates with interest, but the fact remains that it mystifies us to this day in many ways.

I was overtaken by the energies as we walked up the mound and entered the circle, mindful of the constellations of stars beaming down on me. Mesmerizing forces were present, and it felt like we were entering a temporal convergence. I remember taking a picture of one lady as she stood by the stones, and a beam of light was caught on my picture. Many memorable moments came with the experience, and it is one that I hoped to repeat.

After the circle, we were led to the heel stone. It indicates the place on the horizon where the summer solstice sunrise will appear, when viewed from the center of the circle. I hoped to one day return for the autumnal equinox. Arthur Pendragon told me that there were once human remains buried at the bases of many of the stones, which had been taken and boxed up by archeologists and stored in a museum. He asked me if I could get American signatures for a petition to the British government for the return of those remains, considered sacred by the Druids. I said that I would, and I did. I managed to get approximately one thousand signatures from Massachusetts and New York. As of now, the guardians have not been returned to their places, although a court has ordered it. The current struggle is in getting the museum to cooperate with the ruling. However, my heart goes with the Druids and their ongoing fight to get the "guardians" home.

Also on our trip, among many interesting stops, we visited what is known as Woodhenge. Was it older than Stonehenge? Was it inspired by it? I loved seeing it and feeling the vibrations of the area, and I loved wondering about its purpose. It is like discovering more of myself as I explore ancient sites in Great Britain. I remember the lovely moonlight over Woodhenge when we visited it, and it made a lasting impression on my heart.

ANOTHER FORAY INTO THE UK

In 2019, aimed at the summer solstice, I again journeyed to England with my close friend and brother, David Moore. I don't drive, so I really appreciated the freedom of travel we had when we rented a car and he drove us around the country. I cannot even list all of the places we visited, but I will share a few highlights. Although we saw many amazing sites and had spiritual experiences (some of which I will relate here), the most powerful impact on my life this trip had was the connections we made with beautiful people. I was originally invited by Pia Morgan to join her and a few hundred of her friends at an event called Pagan Tribal Gathering (located in Upton, near Nuneaton).

To begin with, I had reserved some space for us in a travelers' boardinghouse with a wonderful lady a friend introduced to me, Susan Marie Paramor. Her kindness and welcoming attitude were a precursor to a beautiful and lasting friendship. She was unimaginably knowledgeable and talented, as a druidic priestess and herbalist, powerful witch, and wise healer, but also a musician, poet, and trained bard. She was a font of knowledge, with an impressive library of druidic information, exclusive information about the renovation of Stonehenge left behind by a historian and Druid, and musical equipment that basically amounted to a fully functional in-home music studio. Her home included a garage apartment inhabited by a lovely man she played music with, a gorgeous yurt outside, and a set of cabins in back near the yurt, in the garden area. The main house, where we stayed, was tastefully decorated, and it felt like home to us. She fed us delicious coffee and toast in the mornings, with jams and jellies she made herself, and delighted us with elderflower champagne and warm hugs. We immediately loved her as a member of our own family, and she was a treasure that keeps shining in our lives to this day. That was only the beginning of the expansion of our hearts in England on this journey.

Stonehenge, 2015

SACRED GROVES AND RITUALS, SPIRITS OF THE LAND

We didn't only enjoy a stay at Susan's home. She also took us to her sacred oak tree at Savernake Forest, on the way to Avebury, and allowed us to commune with it and other ancient trees. She showed us her way of interacting with them, which really touched my heart. We also saw the famous belly oak, and David sat inside it. She went on to share with us her other sacred grove, a grove of powerful and mystical ancient yew trees, located at Hare Warren Wood, near Wilton, and she gave words of caution about their toxic effects and how to be safe in their handling. She informed us that the land there became the property of the first Earl of Pembroke in 1551, given to him along with Wilton Abbey, and they've owned it ever since. She humbled us as she showed us how she treated the queen tree with reverence, doing obeisance to Her, and I will never forget her beautiful songs performed with us in those groves. She taught us a song she was still working on, simply called "The Goddess Song," which was recorded for the first time on Monday, April 19, 2021, while I was finishing this work. I think the name changed at that point to "In the Arms of the Goddess." She is a priestess of the earth, by my reckoning, and with her band, called Car Dia, we watched her perform live. She was such a vision, and her music moved the souls of many. What an enriching experience! She has truly become one of my closest friends today.

While we were at Susan's house, she brought us out back to her yurt and performed a special ritual to dedicate my drum, using fire and water. She had David set up an altar, which he did with faithful reverence, and we brought the drum in and cast our circle. It was a truly heartwarming ritual to share with her in that beautiful space.

Susan was our guide to Stonehenge this trip and also introduced us to other sites and a few groups of Druids. One highlight was when she introduced us to Silbury Hill and the West Kennet Long Barrow while we were on our way to Avebury. We moved along a path through a timeless wheat field to the barrow, and she was an excellent guide, explaining some of the local lore and mystery around Silbury Hill, which we could clearly see from our position just south of it. Wikipedia shares that Silbury Hill is a "prehistoric artificial chalk mound near Avebury. At 39.3 metres (129 feet) high, it is the tallest prehistoric man-made mound in Europe and one of the largest in the world," but the truly fascinating thing was the majickal way she described it. I remember the pictures and feelings in my mind more than her actual words, about how a legend told of a king named Sil, and that he, his horse, and his riches were buried there. Some claim that it is an ancient step pyramid, and there is evidence in that direction as well as a history of human remains being found near its summit. It remains largely a mystery, but it is worth reading about. Susan told me to take a bit of the wheat we were passing, and I did and saved it as a souvenir. King Sil, mentioned above, was legendarily buried there with his horse, and that is where the name comes from—Silbury, meaning where Sil was buried. You can't find these wonderful legends in a simple online search most of the time—but our favorite druidic lady was a font of such knowledge, and she made it come alive for us. She said she had researched that hill for two years while writing a song about it for one of her albums. She even sang it with us.

When we got to the barrow, which had appeared only as a mound of earth and grass to us before, the megalithic stone entrance appeared before us. It was striking, and I was immediately enthralled. We entered this excavated ancient tomb and saw burial chambers to the left and right of us as we proceeded through, all the way to the rear chamber. Some fifty people had been originally interred there, and the spiritual energy could immediately be felt, although their remains had been taken away by the excavators. Susan began to explain a few things about the place to us, always the informative and gentle tour guide, when suddenly I saw a spider on the wall of that last chamber and as quickly was transported outside my normal

West Kennet Long Barrow, 2019

senses into what I can only describe as a dark, spiraling vortex upward. At first, I was afraid that I would be taken away permanently into it, as I felt myself drawn upward, so I asked Susan to take my hand and anchor me there, and she instructed David to do the same. As I flew upward, I encountered pleading spirits of men, women, and children who didn't want to be forgotten, lost in time. They had lived and died here in some tragedy, and my senses were filled with this majickal transportation, their voices, and their faces. While I was having this out-of-body experience, the first of its kind that I can recall ever having, something very different was happening from Susan's and David's point of view. My body seemed to be inhabited by someone larger and stronger than myself, and he was speaking in a deeper voice than mine, in Spanish, to them. They didn't understand much of it, but David (ever the language talent, although his Spanish is rudimentary) is pretty sure he gave them a blessing toward the end. This spirit made a strong impression on them, and as he left my body I returned. I was a bit dazed at first, "phased out" as Susan put it, and she led us back out into the daylight, beginning to dim then, and took a picture of me. She said the picture showed the evidence on my face of what I had just experienced. She confirmed that people often say that back chamber is a "portal." I guess so! I remained completely unaware of the entity who addressed them while I was communing with the spirits until two years later, while working on these memoirs. I was astonished to learn what they had experienced.

While we stayed with Susan and traveled with her, she extended to us her own invitation to a gathering of Druids to take place at Avebury, the largest and arguably oldest stone circle in England, so after the Kennet Long Barrow and a few other stops, we arrived at Avebury near the site for the full-moon ritual. Dennis, who led the rite, and other wonderful people gathered with us at what is called the Moonstone. The rite was beautiful, and somewhat different from the ones we were familiar with in the States.

We were fascinated to learn that there are, in fact, a series of seven stone circles, arranged in a perfectly straight alignment as seen on maps, and Stonehenge appears to be not the largest, and not the oldest. It is composed of some of the largest stones, so perhaps that accounts for its greater fame. Another reason may be that Avebury is in a state of greater ruin, even after some renovation efforts have been made. Avebury, interestingly, is at the center of the seven and is the largest. We found the site charming, and the people even more so. The esbat was truly beautiful, and we were honored to participate.

THE SOLSTICE

The time came for us to join the crowds at Stonehenge for the observation of the summer solstice, and to rendezvous with my friend Arthur Uther Pendragon. Finding that the area we would have preferred to gather in for our work was occupied by food vendors and crowds of partying people from all over the world, and seeing them disrespectfully climbing all over the stones, we were a little put off as we were led away to what is called the heel stone, where we could have some uninterrupted moments for our ritual. As Arthur says, "What you're celebrating, on a mystical level, is that you're looking at light at its strongest. It represents things like the triumph of the king, the power of light over darkness, and just life—life at its fullest."

Arthur led us in the Druid oath of peace, and then he gave me a huge surprise—he officially inducted me into his Loyal Arthurian Warband. He is believed to be the reincarnation of the legendary king of the same name by many, and he had me kneel in the center of our circle. He knighted me, tapping each shoulder with his sword, and welcomed me as a brother. I was so humbled and honored! I will, indeed, be forever loyal to the warband.

While we watched the sun set and walked around, touching the stones of the henge, a group of people, a Welsh tradition of singers and majickal practitioners, all clad in red ceremonial robes, came in to heal the earth with a lovely song/chant for us all to join. As everyone changed their focus and joined them, little by little, it became a powerful spiritual experience for us all. We just kept chanting the beautiful words, many of us singing at our loudest, and a powerful swell of energy was raised. When they released it together, we were all left with a moving spiritual feeling, a greater camaraderie, an unspoken friendship. No matter the diversity of the crowd, no matter how mundane the event had begun, everyone could feel the special difference in our connection with the land after the communal song. Sure, the partiers went right on even after we all left, but we all felt it. Solemn, powerful, and lasting. We bid our esteemed druidic friends goodbye and walked the long trek back to our vehicle.

When it came time to leave our beloved Susan Paramor, we were delighted to learn that she was pretty sure she would drive up and join us at the Pagan Tribal Gathering near Nuneaton! We looked forward to the reunion as we went our way to continue the adventure. There were actually several other excursions we made before the gathering, and the most notable may have been Tintagel.

HOME OF KING ARTHUR?

I was, for some reason, just completely enamored of the Celtic Sea. I knew it would be important to me, but nothing completely prepared me for the powerful feeling of majick in the air there. Merlin's cave, the believed place where the wizard of legend was said to have lived and practiced, was closed due to some renovation work, but we were thrilled to visit castle ruins and see that amazing sea, and nearby we were truly treated to a special experience. At Susan's introduction, we went to the home of a certain Professor Roland Rotherham there in Tintagel, Cornwall.

Professor Rotherham, or Uncle Roly, as we were directed to call him, was perhaps the world's foremost expert on Arthurian legend, having majored in it in university. He was a retired British writer and lecturer, specializing in medieval legends and lore, with special focus on King Arthur, Merlin, and Glastonbury. His Wikipedia entry also mentions his prowess on the topic of historical cookery. He has been introduced as "Professor Roland Rotherham, B.A. (Hons), M.A, Ph.D., Ed.D, M.I.H.G.S, and is said to hold degrees in Ancient and Medieval studies, Anglo-Saxon Culture, Heraldry, Anglo-Norman Culture, Ancient and Medieval Cultural Studies, and Education." A world traveler and having served in the cavalry on the personal staff of Her Majesty the Queen of England, he had a gentlemanly air about him the moment we met him, but he was not at all "stuffy" as one may imagine. Instead, he was kindly, a public servant, and was helping a young woman with a spiritual problem she was facing before he could turn his attention to our visit. He took us over to a nearby Arthurian Hall for a tour of the place where his order met and trained.

Not only was he a member of the Order of the Fellowship of the Knights of the Round Table of King Arthur (a mouthful), but he had a special chair facing the throne in their hall. He occupied a position that was a sort of main advisor to the king in their structure, and he let us know that he had never once sat upon the throne, since it was not allowed for him, although anyone else was encouraged to do so. I took the opportunity to sit on the throne and have a few pictures taken, noting that he stood a respectful distance from it. David felt a kinship with the professor and also declined to sit on the throne. He took us slowly through the hall and then showed us some relics they housed there. Of greatest interest there were detailed scenes in stained glass all around the hall, up high on the walls. He told us that the initiatory and growth process within the order required a careful study of those images, and becoming able to grasp enough information from them to answer very difficult questions about each one was required to advance. As initiates were able to satisfy their instructors on each stained-glass scene, they were able to move to the next one, slowly working their way through the hall. It was a work of years for them rather than hours, and we enjoyed a brief analysis of a few of them with his guidance. One of them featured the Spear of Destiny, and we had fun discussing the history of it with him. He was such a powerful source of information, and we were left with hearts and heads full.

NEW ADVENTURES AND MY FIRST CAMPING EVENT

When we had finally bid our goodbyes and adventured onward from Susan's lovely home, as mentioned above, we looked forward to the gathering. On the way, we passed a sign for Locksley, and David had a fan moment, thinking of Robin Hood. His excitement was even more intense when we passed signs for Sherwood Forest. Perhaps we can explore those in a future visit. When we got to the area near Nuneaton, we found our way to the rustic inn and campsite, owned by Chris and Dee White, a lovely couple who worked hard at catering to guests and maintaining the site. Their hospitality was second to none, and I would definitely love to return. I'm not a camper, so I was grateful for the nice accommodations offered to us in the inn and then the house. While at the gathering, my main function there was to give my Teatime with the Cabots traditional talk, using a PowerPoint presentation in a small concert hall named Joey's Bar. It was a cozy space and ended up completely packed with enthusiastic listeners, with standing room only as we progressed. I was honored to share my message with them all. David did a small workshop on empathy a bit later during the event, and it was well received.

While we were there, I was surprised to be asked to perform a handfasting at the bonfire area. I am accustomed to preparing ahead of time, but I was properly trained and quite experienced, so I accepted the task and decided to wing it. To my delight, not only did it flow well, but the onlookers were amazed at the energy and vibrational quality of the rite. They were murmuring about how wonderful it was for some time after, and I was happy to see the excited young couple as they joined their lives together. What a special way to build a connection to the people and the land, and to represent the Cabot tradition on English soil! I knew my Reverend Mother Laurie Cabot would be proud if she was there.

THE LOVELY SORITA

I purposefully saved a major highlight of my second trip to England for last. I wanted to share it now, pointing toward this book's "Afterthoughts" section. While traveling to various locations and then returning to Susan's, during our first week there we went to Glastonbury. We were able to connect with Sorita d'Este, a well-known author and High Priestess of the Alexandrian Tradition, and a devotee of Hekate. Sorita was a ray of sunshine on our trip, and she enthusiastically escorted us (and even bought our entry) to the beautiful Chalice Wells. We marveled at the quiet, contemplative culture there, and the solemn attitude of the people who came to silently pray or meditate there. We took pictures and gently discussed the history there, made offerings in one of the wells, and then decided we had to see the Glastonbury Tor, while we had our local guide at hand (at her suggestion, of course), and we did. When we saw the tor, it really did have a certain majestic feel to it. It's what is left of an old church built high on that hill, and Sorita gave us the history from her expansive knowledge of local lore. Then we got quite a surprise after descending the hill—she and her man owned land right there in the shadow of the tor, and they were growing lovely plants on it. She led us to a circle they had there, then shared some information about the plant life around us. I look forward to seeing what they continue to do with that plot of land as time goes by—it was off to a lovely start. We were invited to her home, met her kindly son and lovely cat, and got a tour of her famous garden. She is a valuable resource to the community, and an important elder in the Pagan movement by my reckoning, and I count myself fortunate to make her acquaintance. Since the trip, she and I have become close friends, and I treasure her.

Sorita d'Este and I at the Chalice Wells, Glastonbury, England, 2019

IRELAND

The Emerald Isle, as they say! As a boy, my fascination with Ireland was so intense because of its holiday here in America, Saint Patrick's Day, and the Irish culture that played a part in sewing the fabric of this great nation. I learned stories about fairies and leprechauns, contributing to one of my favorite colors being green.

This opened my spiritual eye on the Goddess Bride, or Brigid (there have been various spellings). In my native culture, we too celebrate February 2 or Imbolc/Imbolg as "Día de la Candelaria," associated with Afro-Cuban Oya. It always linked, to me, with feminine divinity.

My trip to Ireland in 2024 was preceded by years of anticipation, and that allowed me to reflect on my roots and spirituality. I believe that nothing is coincidental. Not merely a vacation, for me it became a spiritual pilgrimage, one full of manifestation and revelation. It meant growth for me, a humble being who has his heart on earth, humanity, love, and spirituality. I was to feel the heartbeat of the Mother there.

THE HILL OF TARA AND THE HILL OF SLANE

My first visit to the Hill of Tara was one filled with wonder and amazement. I recall, as I walked along the trail to Tara with my boyfriend from Washington, DC, and my dear friend from Salisbury, England, I was filled with a thrilling and meaningful energy. Alex is Christian, but he is very supportive of my very different religious path. Susan Marie Paramor is a bard, a druidic high priestess, and she and I have always had a similar devotional path when it comes to ancestral worship. As we began our adventure, I had a moment when I felt a portal of spiritual awakening as if I was going back in time. I was washed with elements of fresh air, moist earth, and lush green, and it awoke my third eye. I felt like I was walking through the air. It's easy to tell that this place was an important site of kings, warriors, and tales of Gods and Goddesses. It felt like we were walking on legends themselves, a bit surreal as if stepping into a magickal movie screen and joining the characters.

I was there for our celebration of the spring equinox. This was a public place with many tourists, but we planned to internally create a ritual experience for ourselves, just holding hands and casting a circle silently in our minds. It was such an honor to do this with people so dear to me. I was focused on reverence and honor, devotion and magick with these wonderful friends. The slippery slopes of the banks were so muddy that, for a second, Susan and I (the priest and priestess) fell face down and kissed the ground, making it a memorable moment full of laughter. We definitely felt energetic elation.

Afterward, we went to the Hill of Slane, and I learned some of the history of these two hills. You may have heard the story of how Patrick defeated the Pagan Druids and asserted Christian dominance over the area, but when I visited these hills, I felt drawn to earlier times, when the Druids performed sacred rites on these hills especially at this time of year, for the spring equinox. The High King would light a fire on the hill originally, and it was the original Pagan history of the place that resonated with me most. Learning the story of one of the oldest kings in Ireland, Sláine, and how he was buried on this hill, giving it its name, I understood that the rite was honoring his memory, among other things. I could feel a spiritual connection, since Celtic blood runs through my veins, and the story of the connection of these two hills seemed personally meaningful to me.

THE FELLOWSHIP OF ISIS AND HUNTINGTON CASTLE

As we approached the castle for the weekend, I was open and innocent, feeling a bit like a tourist for a moment, and not knowing what was in store for me.

A revelation and some notable paranormal activity was the highlight for that weekend. *Nothing is coincidental,* I kept thinking. We were at the castle by invitation from the head of the Order of Bards, Ovates & Druids (OBOD), who also runs the Fellowship of Isis at the same location in Clonegal, Ireland, at this magnificent Huntington Castle, keeping Olivia Robertson's mission alive. It was Susan's many connections that brought us to this magickal castle and the pilgrimage to the Temple of Isis. It felt as if much of my life had led to this time, and the anticipation was electric.

Olivia Melian Durden-Robertson *(right)* and Laurence Durden-Robertson *(left)*, Fellowship of Isis

MY IRISH REVELATION

I woke up with joy in my heart, not knowing what was about to happen. I remember getting ready for breakfast and thinking how wonderful it was to be in the castle of the Robertsons, and to get a feel for the legend that Olivia left behind. At a moment when I was putting on my boots, the vanity mirror that revolves moved slowly on its own. I stopped in surprise and thought it was odd. I tried to think of a physical explanation for how that mirror could have moved. There was no discernable air movement or vibration. Drawing a blank on that, I then wondered about a spiritual reason, thinking that maybe it could be a sign from Olivia and Laurence of their presence and acceptance. That thought definitely warmed my heart. What magick resided within those walls!

We all started congregating by the courtyard, Druids and other practitioners alike. I was greeted warmly by all as they were amazed by my visit from America and my first time in Ireland. The procession started in the late morning as we went to Olivia's favorite rose garden, where the pleasant smell was unbelievable, and it really filled my senses. It cannot be said that this New Yorker never stops to smell the roses! My friend Susan sang her "Goddess Song," which further set the mood for us all. We then headed into a cedar grove that was planted around the time of Olivia's birth (so a little over a hundred years before this day). There was a circular opening inside these magnificent trees, and we gathered and circled around. Each of us took a turn saying a little something from the heart, and then we had a moment of quiet meditation. I had an immediate and powerful vision.

First, I saw a Goddess walking toward me in a mist, coming from the inner core of the trees before me. I could see her just from the waist down, at first just a silhouette, glowing. As she took each step, she seemed to change from one Goddess to another, as if to show me that her many avatars are all just one Lady. This was unique, because all of my previous visions of Goddess had begun with her having a silver glow, but this time it was a golden glow, growing brighter, and there was something special and new about the feeling that washed over me. I was stunned, as she walked directly to me with purpose. I could just make out that her appearance, including her clothing and other adornment, would change each time she stepped, but as she drew nearer, the details seemed clearer and clearer. Although she walked, she was floating in the ether rather than appearing to walk upon the ground. The light was warm and radiant, and, as the details grew clearer, I could see that she was holding a chalice. I knew that she carried the waters of life in that chalice, and she was beckoning to me, giving the water to me. She was gesturing toward me with it in a very familiar way, as if to say to me, "May you never thirst." I was so humbled in Her presence, and I knew that this was no mere vision. I felt clear understanding of this message, and the light was so beautiful, even if a little blinding. Even when she drew so close that it was as if I could touch her, the light made it difficult to make out enough detail of her appearance for me to describe it now.

At that moment, we all ended the meditation, and I woke to normal consciousness. We headed toward the temple together, and I felt a contented calmness, mixed with amazement and gratitude. Our precession entered the lower level of the castle. We headed directly toward the well at its center. The hall led to a large, rectangular room, with the well at its left corner, and we gathered near the well, facing it. As I was a guest from abroad, they had me sit in front of the group in the narrow area leading to the well, up front with Susan, on the ancient stone floor. The majority of us had lined up on the sides of the passage. The High Priestess spoke, mentioning many Goddesses related to the springtime, since we were there to observe the spring equinox. I recall that she mentioned Rhiannon, Brigid, and a Goddess of poetry, fertility, and knowledge, the Goddess associated with the creation of the River Boyne, called Boann. She spoke of Danu as well. They asked me to speak in honor and veneration of a Goddess, and I surprised them by deviating from the norm and speaking of the Crone Goddess called the Cailleach. They had all been focused on springtime maiden aspects of Goddess, but in my personal devotional practice, I have always honored the crone aspect of my Goddess as well. It brought knowing and pleasantly surprised smiles from everyone. As soon as we had all spoken our blessings and messages of honor and gratitude, the High Priestess, who was standing at the well, went down into it and drew water from it. She came out and gave the water to me, and I was filled with the feeling that this mirrored my vision. I felt that the gesture of her giving me that water was exactly correlated to the Goddess giving me the chalice earlier. I teared up and was overwhelmed with gratitude and recognition. My spiritual sensations were beyond words that I can share on this page. I was literally given the waters of life, and the High Priestess was certainly a vessel of our Goddess, even as her vessel carried the waters from the well. This was a magnificent revelation, an epiphany of sorts, and I'll never forget it so long as I live.

We stood up and turned right to face the rest of the chamber, and there was an altar on the far wall. We moved toward it, gathering as closely as we could. Another High Priestess was sitting there. We were told that she had been there, deep in meditation, for about an hour. They announced that "the Oracle will speak." She spoke of our Lady's splendor, of the beauty and gift of the earth. She channeled our Goddess and spoke of how humans are treating that world, and the ramifications of our adverse actions against it, but assured us that she will always protect her children. We were sitting on pillows that had been placed on stone blocks and soaking up all of Her words. One of the young men from our precession was then to speak, but he was shy in our presence, so they brought me to the altar to speak in his stead. I felt extremely sentimental, and tears flowed as I expressed to them that nothing is coincidence. I said that I was there because our Lady had intentionally brought me there, and I felt that her reasons for having me there as Her guest had become clear. I felt an ancestral pull, and there was a feeling of coming full circle, a feeling of global connection to Her. I spoke of how this was no mere visit, but truly a pilgrimage on my journey of service to Her. I brought everyone's attention to the legacy that Olivia and Laurence had built, with great reverence. I not only felt welcomed by their grandnephew (who maintains the estate today) but felt spiritually welcomed by them directly. I said, "This morning, something odd happened to me. While I was getting ready, I had the sensation that I was in a legendary place, wrought by their hands in a manner of speaking, and a deep appreciation settled in my heart for all that they had done." I told them about the mirror moving on its own, and how it made me feel.

This place had a fascinating history. There is a well in the center of it, and it was built first. The castle was a product of fortification built around this well, which has been a recurring theme in ancient building practices. Protecting the source of water made sense, since it was the most precious life-giving resource. If it hadn't been protected, it would be intentionally contaminated by enemies. This protection was vital; if there were soldiers fighting for the castle's safety, at least they had fresh water. In cases of siege, a good water source meant the difference between life and death for its inhabitants. The grateful residents treated it with great reverent care.

First, an abbey was built around the well. It was built again and again there, and eventually the castle fortifications were built around it. It was added to over many years, and that resulted in the estate we were visiting in our modern day. Seeing the evidence of the growth of this impressive construction and its rich history ignited my sense of wonder further. After so many stages of addition, it is currently more than twice the size it originally was, they told us.

A FINAL THOUGHT

Throughout my many years of spiritual development, I've cherished some key points of wisdom. Among the most significant to me is understanding that spirituality is rooted in humility rather than an inflated ego. The term "ego" describes our perception of self, influencing our decision-making abilities. A balanced self-view, fostering confidence and sound judgment, is crucial for mental and emotional well-being. However, to access a higher power for soul purification, humility is essential. To approach divinity, we must transcend ourselves, embracing authenticity, gratitude, and genuine demeanor. Otherwise, we impede our own progress. This notion defines my personal existence, granting me purpose and standing as my utmost priority. One may not approach the divine with false motives or arrogance.

NEW YORK COVEN OF WITCHES, 9/11 REMEMBRANCE GATHERING

I was recently asked to give a speech to our beloved coven in New York, as we gathered in remembrance of those we lost in the events on September 11, 2001. It was a solemn occasion, and I accepted this responsibility. As I feel that this was an important moment in my life and in my interaction with my longtime affiliated coven, I want to share it here and ask that you, dear reader, reflect on where you were and how you felt during and after this tragic set of events. Moving forward, what are your wishes for New York and for the world?

The autumn equinox, marking my solar return, often became a celebration shared between Salem, Massachusetts, with Laurie and the temple, and the "New York Coven of Witches." Lady Rhea hosted her "New York City Meetups" at the old Enchantments, now known as The Immigrant. During one such Sabbat, the *New York Times* featured an article on the coven, and I was requested to lead a commemoration for 9/11, giving a speech that our coven and the media could draw upon. It was to reflect my sentiments and personal history and my thoughts focused on this tragic incident that impacted every New Yorker profoundly.

> "Let us embrace this moment of silence as we delve into our individual experiences of 9/11, and then I will share mine . . .
>
> When I ponder upon the tragic events of 9/11 in this remarkable city of New York, I do so with deep reverence for the city and this country, acknowledging my unique bond to them both. This country offered me the freedom of democracy and an escape from Fidel Castro's Communist regime that my family and I sought refuge from. Knowing that I was a part of our family's exodus from what felt to them like a new hell and into the United States proved transformative for me, significantly shaping my spiritual journey as chronicled in my book *Memoirs of a High Priest*.
>
> Countless New Yorkers bore witness to the devastation of 9/11, each embedded with permanent impressions of a distinct experience. My own account feels surreal, having been an eyewitness to the destroyed building site after I was evacuated from a nearby federal building. I absorbed the shock and despair, energies that lingered for years.
>
> Our city changed irreversibly, but its people forged a new bond, cultivating a shared sense of unity and compassion. Our spirits underwent transformation; we who survived this tragedy were standing together as human beings, any divisions between us forgotten.
>
> With time, our emotional wounds will fade for future generations, but the erected monuments stand as eternal reminders, honoring each life lost. They symbolize respect and dignity for those departed souls. Already, in this moment, I can barely detect the surface of the energies that once pervaded that fateful day. Our city and nation continue to heal from the many effects of this human tragedy.
>
> As a devotee of the Goddess, I believe that the path to healing is unfolded through exposure to light, knowledge, truth, and love. I hereby extend blessings for New York City's continued growth amid its trials, and I invoke divine blessings for its continued betterment. May our collective experiences and emotions merge and harmonize, ensuring the authenticity of our collective historical account. The memory of 9/11 shall never fade. New York City and this nation remain my sanctuary! May the Lord and Lady guide us toward an enduring victory of love!"

MORE TO COME

What adventures are left to come? How will I find new ways to serve my Goddess? This is the second edition, but perhaps a later, updated version of this book will become available as well. How have you been touched by Goddess? Let us all honor Her in our lives.

To our Goddess Omnipotent, I now conclude these spiritual memoirs with the following words:

Mighty Mother,
Always with me
From the beginning
Until the end,
I honor thee
Through my life's service.
So shall it be!

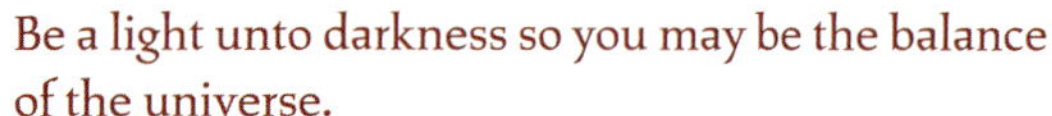

Be a light unto darkness so you may be the balance of the universe.

—Reverend High Priest Alexander Cabot

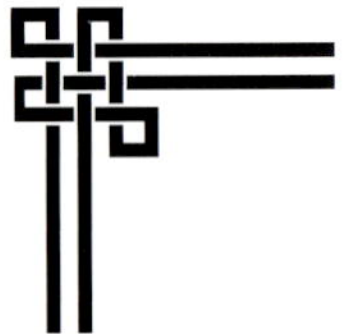

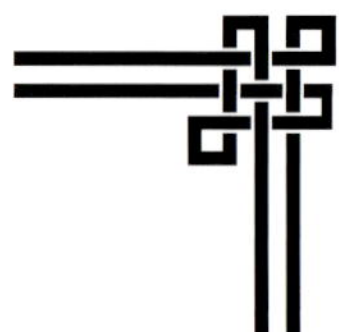

AFTERTHOUGHTS

BY SORITA D'ESTE

As an author and publisher, I learned a long time ago that the story of a book does not start with the opening lines, nor does it finish with the last few words. Books have the potential to transform both their writers and their readers considerably. The writer is transformed through the process of conveying their knowledge and experience, pondering the importance of their experiences and encounters. Alexander has done a terrific job of carefully and respectfully curating and sharing aspects of his journey that were essential to him, which he felt would benefit future generations. As readers, all we have to do is invest a few hours of reading through these chapters, and we can—if we are open and ready for it—gain insights and perspectives that will help us navigate our own pathways through the mysteries.

There is no doubt about it—books are teachers, and in the world of esotericism, books may well be the *greatest* of teachers. They are silent leaders with the ability to educate and transform our lives, and alongside that, our knowledge and understanding. They can bring learning to readers anywhere in the world, and they can overcome linguistic barriers through translation. This book, which you now hold in your hands, is a delightful experiential journey through the mystical and magical life of a lovely priest, whose integrity and warmth is undeniably beautiful and magical. You just absorbed an exceptional insight into aspects of both the Wiccan and Pagan scene in the USA over the last few decades, and you got private peeks into Cuban and African diaspora cultures that influenced Alexander. The diversity of experience and the value and respect he has always applied to his teachers and practices are some of the reasons I feel an affinity for Alexander and value him as a friend.

Like Alexander, I was influenced by various spiritual traditions, and like his, my journey started somewhere culturally and religiously very different from where I live now. I was born in South Africa, with primarily European ancestors, raised in a mix of South African and Italian culture. I moved to the UK more than twenty-five years ago, but having experienced different perspectives on religion and culture, not only through the country of my birth but also by my experiences elsewhere, I am diverse.

Through my work as an author, I have been privileged to spend the last twenty or so years of my life studying the traditions and mythologies of many world religions. I have been able to visit some of the most famous sacred sites of both modern and ancient religions worldwide, and I have spent time along the way with practitioners of many different religious and magical traditions. In addition, through my everyday life as an esoteric publisher, my work life is filled with making the writings of others available to the world. It has given me a vantage point that is sometimes strikingly different from that of my peers, but one that I value every step of the way.

As a UK-based practitioner, it was not until recent years that I have gained an understanding, of sorts, of the complexities and size of the Goddess and Wiccan movement in the USA. Overall, the British occult and Pagan groups are, perhaps, a lot more reserved and private than those I have encountered in the USA, although there are always exceptions on both sides. I continue to be astonished at the diversity and dedication shown by practitioners in the USA and the level of professionalism of US-based practitioners and teachers!

The origins of the practices of Wicca, which I explored in the book *Wicca: Magickal Beginnings* (2008, coauthored with Rankine), can be traced back to the medieval grimoires, the Renaissance, and practices found throughout the ancient Mediterranean, with some influences echoed in those found in ancient Egypt and Babylon. Gerald Gardner's Wicca movement may have started in the UK, but it was transformed in the USA over the last few decades into the global movement it has become today. It is now an international religion with many different facets, initiatory and not, and it has given birth to many of the Pagan and Goddess traditions that took their inspiration from the practices, core beliefs, and celebrations of Wicca. Wicca, as a magical and religious tradition, continues to evolve at the hands of each and every practitioner or group who practice it, and who bring their own experience and knowledge to it. Magic, no matter when, takes on the religion of its age. It is alive and continues to evolve and transform.

That is evidenced in the magical practices and beliefs coalesced at the hands of Gerald Gardner in the UK during the 1950s. Gardner's work was inspired and informed by his experience with the New Forest coven, as well as the work of the occultist Aleister Crowley, the American folklorist Charles G. Leland, and many others who went before. Crowley and Leland were, likewise, influenced by what went before. Crowley's work was built on his knowledge of the Hermetic Order of the Golden Dawn, the work of Eliphas Levi, and that of countless others—not to mention his own experiences and experiments. Leland, on the other hand, was informed by the writings of previous generations and informants in the regions he traveled. With each generation, we find the same. For example, Eliphas Levi was influenced by writers such as Fludd, Paracelsus, Swedenborg, and many others.

Today, it is perhaps simpler than ever to record and share the knowledge and experiences we have gained, but it is always a labor of love. When it is done in the way that Alexander has in this book, it is also an act of devotion and service. It might be cliché, but it is true in every way that studying the past can help us learn from the successes and failures of those who went before us, and then in turn to continue the work of improving and evolving that knowledge for a brighter and better future. Alexander has done so beautifully in this tome. I hope you will embrace it and take from it, as I have, the passion, love, and respect the author has for the teachers and experiences he has had in his life, and also find ways to apply it in your own life.

Many blessings on your path,

—Sorita d'Este
Glastonbury, 2021

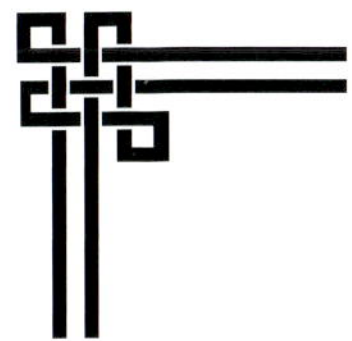
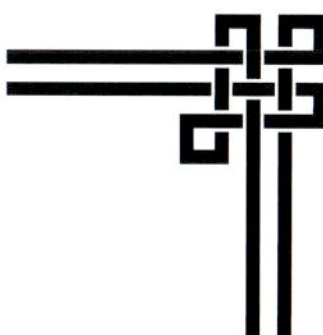

BIBLIOGRAPHY

https://babblingbrookereadings.com/rolla-nordic/. Retrieved from the web on January 23, 2023.

http://oconsolador.com/linkfixo/biografias/ingles/amalia.html. Retrieved from the web on March 14, 2023.

Ayegboyin, Deji, and S. K. Olajide. "Olodumare." *Encyclopedia of African Religion*. SAGE, 2009.

"BBC Inside Out—Sybil Leek; White Witch." BBC, October 28, 2002.

Bulfinch. *One Hundred Saints*. Boston: Little, Brown, 2001.

Cabot, Laurie. *The Power of the Witch: The Earth, the Moon, and the Magical Path to Enlightenment*.

Cabot, Laurie. *Book of Shadows*.

Carlson, Maria. *No Religion Higher Than Truth: A History of the Theosophical Movement in Russia, 1875–1922*. Princeton University Press, 2015.

"Creole." *The Encyclopedia Britannica*. March 1, 2019.

Crowley, Aleister. *Crowley's Book of the Law*.

Crowley, Aleister. *Moon Child*.

Crowley, Aleister. *The Qabbalah of Aleister Crowley*.

Dann, Graham M. S. "Religion and Cultural Identity: The Case of Umbanda." *Sociological Analysis* 30, no. 3 (1979): pp. 208–25.

Daugherty, Michelle. "Kemetism–Ancient Religions in Our Modern World." Michigan State University, October 2, 2014.

Dawes, Gregory. "The Rationality of Renaissance Magic."

Doyle, Arthur Conan. "The Most Important Thing in the World." https://arthurconandoyle.co.uk/spiritualist.

Edward-Ekpu, Uwagbale. "Why So Many African Americans Have Nigerian Ancestry." Quartz, Business News, August 10, 2020. https://qz.com/africa/1890291/why-so-many-african-americans-have-nigerian-ancestry/.

"The Devil`s Blue Dye: Indigo and Slavery." April 21, 2018.

González-Wippler, Migene. *Santeria: The Religion*. Llewellyn, 2003.

Hancock, Graham. *The Sign and the Seal—the Quest for the Lost Ark of the Covenant.*

Harrison, P. M. *Profane Egyptologists: The Revival and Reconstruction of Ancient Egyptian Religion*. UCL (University College London), 2012.

Heiser, James D. *Prisci Theologi and the Hermetic Reformation in the Fifteenth Century*. Repristination, 2011.

"Hermeticism." *The Concise Oxford Dictionary of World Religions.*

Jacob, Margaret. *The Origins of Freemasonry. Facts and Fictions.* Philadelphia: University of Pennsylvania Press, 2006.

Kardec, Allan. *The Spirit's Book*. 1857.

Kardec, Allan. *The Genesis According to Spiritism*. 1868.

LaVey, Anton Szandor. *Satanic Bible*. 2017.

Louagie, Kimberly. "The Bonds He Did Not Break: Harry Houdini and Wisconsin." Wisconsin Magazine of History 85, no. 3 (Spring 2002): 2–17.

Lovecraft, H. P. *Necronomicon*. 2008.

Lux, Ferre. "Doyle, Sir Arthur Conan." Occult World, June 30, 2017. https://occult-world.com/doyle-sir-arthur-conan/.

Marshall, Peter. *The Philosopher's Stone: A Quest for the Secrets of Alchemy*. 2001.

Mathiesen, Robert, and Theitic. *The Rede of the Wiccae: Adriana Porter, Gwen Thompson and the Birth of a Tradition of Witchcraft*. 2005.

Mayo, Caswell A. *American Druggist and Pharmaceutical Record*, 1902.

McKinley, Catherine E. *Indigo: In Search of the Color That Seduced the World.* 2011.

"Order of the Eastern Star," *Masonic Dictionary*, retrieved January 9, 2013.

Peel, J. Y. L. "The Three Circles of Yoruba Religion." University of California Press, 2016 (214–32).

Villarreal, Raul, and Rene Villarreal. *Hemingway's Cuban Son: Reflections on the Writer by His Long Time Majordomo*. 2008.

Ruggeri, Amanda. "The Lost History of the Freemasons." BBC, February 24, 2022. http://www.bbc.com/travel/story/20161209-secret-history-of-the-freemasons-in-scotland.

Sanchez, Sara. *Afro-Cuban Diasporan Religions: A Comparative Analysis of the Literature and Selected Annotated Bibliography*. 2000.

Schwartz, Stephan A. "Spirit World." *American Heritage*, April/May 2005.

Smith, Robert Sydney. *Kingdoms of the Yoruba*. University of Wisconsin Press, 1988.

Spence, Lewis. (2003). *Encyclopedia of Occultism and Parapsychology*. Kessinger, 2003 (491).

Szonyi, Gyorgy E. *John Dee's Occultism: Magical Exaltation Through Powerful Signs*. SUNY Series in Western Esoteric Traditions. State University of New York Press, 2005.

Three Initiates. *The Kybalion: A Study of the Hermetic Philosophy of Ancient Egypt and Greece*. Rough Draft Printing, 2012.

Wigington, Patti. "The History of a Year and a Day in Paganism." Learn Religions, August 26, 2020. learnreligions.com/year-and-a-day-2561939.